The Cruelty of Heresy

By the same author
Fear, Love and Worship
Guilt, Anger and God
The Rise of Moralism

The Cruelty of Heresy

An Affirmation of Christian Orthodoxy

C. FitzSimons Allison

MOREHOUSE PUBLISHING
Harrisburg, PA

Second Printing, 1994

Unless otherwise noted, all Scripture quotations are from the Revised Standard Version, copyright © 1946, 1952, © 1971, 1973 by the Division of Christian Education of the National Council of Churches of Christ in the USA.

Morehouse Publishing
P.O. Box 1321
Harrisburg, PA 17105

Library of Congress Cataloging-in-Publication Data
Allison, C. FitzSimons (Christopher FitzSimons), 1927-
  The cruelty of heresy: an affirmation of christian orthodoxy / C. FitzSimons Allison.
    p. cm.
  Includes bibliographical references and index.
  ISBN 0-8192-1513-9 (pbk.)
  1. Heresies, Christian—History—Early church, ca. 30-600.
2. Apologetics—20th century. I. Title.
BT1319.A45 1994   93-39541
273—dc20   CIP

Printed in the United States of America
by BSC LITHO
Harrisburg, PA 17105

For
the Congregation of Grace Church, New York City
who taught me much of what grace means
and
Christopher FitzSimons Allison, Jr.

Χριστο φερω (Christopher, *Christ-bearer*)
το ονομα ημων και το αιματε ημων
κατα σαρκα συτωσ λογιζηται ινα και
ονομα και αιμα ηται κατα πνευμα
εισ το Χριστον ημιν φερειν ωσ αυτον
φερει ημιν.

That our name and blood according to the flesh
may be so reckoned
that both name and blood be according to the Spirit
as we bear Christ who bears us.

Contents

Foreword by the Archbishop of Canterbury 9

Preface 11

Acknowledgments . . . . : 13

Introduction 15

1 Short Beds and Narrow Blankets 25

2 Attacks on Christian Faith 49

3 The Trinity 67

4 Arianism: The Three Deities 81

5 The Cappadocians 95

6 Apollinarianism 105

7 Nestorianism: The Train of Salvation
    Does Not Stop for Sinners 119

8 Eutychianism: The Religious Withering
    of Humanity 139

9 A Rectitude of the Heart 153

10 Orthodoxy and Pagan Religions Revived 165

Notes 179

Bibliography 187

Index 191

Foreword

The identity of a Church comes not only from its changing historical and cultural forms but pre-eminently—some of us will argue—from what it believes. The early Church established its teaching about the Person of Christ and the Trinity in the famous four Councils of Nicaea, Constantinople, Ephesus and Chalcedon. The victory did not come easily. Orthodoxy was challenged by deviant teachings presented by attractive and sincere apologists. Such heresies were examined and found wanting. The Creeds of the Four Councils have since formed the faith and the mind of the universal Church with its cornerstone being the uniqueness of Jesus Christ as Son of God and Saviour.

But this teaching is under attack again. Plausible, but ultimately superficial, teachings both from within and outside the Church force us to re-examine the place of Jesus Christ and the doctrine of the Trinity. Isn't it time, we are being urged, for the Church in this pluralist age to accommodate itself to a world in which Christianity is just one religion among many? Isn't Jesus just one among many "Saviours"? Isn't it time to recognize "truth" in heresy and "heresy" in orthodoxy?

In this timely and well written book Bishop Christopher FitzSimons Allison examines the way the faith of the Church is challenged today by heresies which threaten its very being. I cannot think of very many people better equipped to write such a book. Bishop Allison is a scholar of distinction well known for his search for truth and his thoroughness of research. But his career as a pastor at Grace Church, New York as well as Bishop of South Carolina, also reveals his enviable abilities to communicate abstruse theological ideas in forms that inter-mesh with the experience of Christians struggling to live out their faith in the real world. The interpenetration of scholarship and parochial experience in the Bishop's life show that the two are not in competition.

Bishop Allison's book is surely ideal for two groups of readers. First, for intelligent lay Christians who are mystified and disturbed by attempts to jettison key doctrines of the faith. They will be edified by a book that makes doctrine accessible with illustrations from ordinary life which they will recognize. The other main group is the theological student and minister of religion. It is rare to find a book about the history of doctrine which is so concerned about the mission and growth of the Church. Bishop Allison identifies with this group too. He shows that current "heresies" around today, however culturally attractive they may be, actually debilitate the Church's mission and lead to decline. Such heresies in the long run, he argues, are actually cruel because instead of leading to faith and life they end in doubt and death.

It is equally important to recognize that Bishop Allison's argument is not that arch-conservatism is the only way forward. This would be to underestimate his concern for truth as well as his commitment to relevance. The charitable, thoughtful and courteous way in which "heresy" is presented reveals the Bishop's awareness that deviant teachings often spring from a deep commitment to the Christian faith. He is prepared to listen to their search for truth. However, he points out that when Jesus Christ is not seen as "the way, the truth and the life" such teachings fall far short of the fullness of the Christian truth and ultimately distort its message.

In the Church of England at every Ordination service and every fresh ministry the minister or priest has to commit himself or herself to the "faith of the Church which is 'revealed' in Holy Scripture and 'expressed' in the Catholic Creeds . . . which faith the Church is called to proclaim afresh in each generation." Bishop Allison's book falls splendidly in this Anglican tradition. For this reason I am most happy to commend his relevant challenge to the modern Church.

George Carey
Archbishop of Canterbury
Lambeth Palace
London

Preface

Professor Leonard Hodgson was fond of telling his students how important it was to learn what kind of god people don't believe in. Proclamation of the gospel must always involve a witness to God who is frequently quite different from the gods humans imagine.

I am unashamed of the enthusiasm for othodoxy that I share with Dorothy Sayers who believed "there was never anything so perilous or so exciting as orthodoxy, nothing so sane and so thrilling."

This enthusiasm is born perversely not from virtue but from sin. I find John Calvin's commentary on 1 Tim. 1:19 to be enduringly accurate. "All errors that have existed in the Christian Church from the beginning, proceeded from this source, that in some persons, ambition, and in others, covetousness, extinguished the true fear of God. A bad conscience is, therefore, the mother of all heresies . . ." Unless guided by the Church's creeds and Councils, I believe I would produce the most virulent heretical distortions of scripture. This recognition stems from a humility, however inadequate, that I would be delighted to share with those whose confidence in themselves leads them to devalue the creeds and Councils.

Luther once observed: "In domestic affairs, I defer to Katie.

11

Otherwise, I am led by the Holy Ghost!" Readers of this book are benefited more than they know by the fact that deference to my wife, Martha, is not by any means relegated to domestic affairs. Her diligent help and wise criticism have been marked by that unusual quality of patience that is untainted by compliance. For this the readers have reason to be grateful.

I am indebted to so many teachers, colleagues, students, and parishioners, who have been the occasions and means by which I have been enabled to begin to understand and appreciate the profound teachings of the Councils, that it is impossible to thank them adequately. I would, however, like to express my deepest gratitude to Professor Stephen Smith and to the Rev. Fleming Rutledge who have each taken a great deal of trouble to help me make this material accessible and readable.

Christopher FitzSimons Allison
Georgetown, SC
1993

Acknowledgments

The author would like to thank the publishers, editors and authors of the following publications for their kind permission to quote from copyrighted materials:

Quotations from *Speaking the Christian God,* Alvin Kimel, editor, © 1992, Wm. B. Eerdmans Publishing.

Excerpt from *Truth to Tell: The Gospel as Public Trust* by Lesslie Newbigin, © 1991, Wm. B. Eerdmans Publishing.

Excerpts reprinted from *Christological Controversy* by Richard A. Norris, copyright © 1980 Fortress Press. Used by permission of Augsburg Fortress.

Quotation from *Sex, Money and Power* by Philip Turner, © 1985, Cowley Publications.

Quotation from *For the Time Being* by W. H. Auden copyright © 1945 by W. H. Auden. Reprinted by permission of Random House, Inc.

Excerpt from C. S. Lewis' Introduction to *On the Incarnation* by Saint Athanasius, copyright © 1946 by the Macmillan Publishing Company.

Quotation from *Systematic Theology* by Paul Tillich, © 1963 by the University of Chicago Press.

Introduction

A belief that human society is part of a universe in which order is assured by the might and benefi-cence of its Creator may legitimately be reflected in an assumption that men are assured of their desserts. Even where faith in a divinely ordered universe has been shaken, many have continued to believe in the possibility and in the desirability of such justice and have sought it with fervour; when, however, as sense of order in the universe is not merely shaken but ceases to exist, and when, in the resulting chaos, men see themselves as flotsam without recognisable obligations or hopes of due reward, then justice becomes a chimera.[1]

Honor Matthews

Things fall apart; the center cannot hold;
Mere anarchy is loosed upon the world,
The blood-dimmed tide is loosed, and everywhere
The ceremony of innocence is drowned . . .[2]

W. B. Yeats

15

A sense of disorder pervades our culture and our churches. Poets and playwrights have been telling us for some time that our society no longer has a stable center or firm foundation and it is now apparent in our social and political consciousness. There seem to be few agreed boundaries, limits, or teachings and the Christian church's traditional role in providing them for much of Western society is weaker today than at any time in many centuries. Attempted alternatives to Christianity have failed to provide the underlying sustenance. How should Christians begin to address this situation? We have long neglected a real treasure of the Christian faith: the classical guidelines for knowing Father, Son, and Holy Spirit, one God. These teachings preserved the power and uniqueness of the Christian faith and they can be again a means by which we can recover the knowledge of who God is at the center and foundation of our lives and our society.

The unparalleled achievements of the Christian Church in the fourth and fifth centuries forged the arena within which the great mysteries of the Trinity and the divine and human natures of Christ were preserved from dissipation among the myriad gods and religions of the ancient world. At the same time these achievements in creeds and Councils still provide the link to those roots of Christian vitality through which we can recover what has been the center of our civilization and the goal of our lives.

The achievements of the first four General or Ecumenical Councils have continued to serve as guidelines for Roman Catholic, Eastern Orthodox, Anglican, Reformed, Lutheran, and Methodist churches. Not since the early centuries have they been under as serious assault as they are today both from without and from within the churches.

These guidelines for Christian orthodoxy laid down in these Councils, have become virtually a private and arcane preserve of professional theologians and historians whose endeavors are increasingly ignored by rank and file Christians. These important issues too frequently are treated in a merely academic way with no reference to their implications for human life. At the same time, some excellent scholarly contributions urgently need to be made accessible to ordinary Christians and to those who are skeptical of Christianity itself.

Trying to communicate this important material to students led me to ask the question, "What happens to someone who follows heretical teachings?" It became quickly and readily apparent how cruel heretical teachings are and how prevalent the heresies are in contemporary times. Victims of these teachings have been encouraged either to escape the world and their basic humanity into some form of flight and death or to use religion to undergird and isolate further their own self-centered self from the need to be loved and to love.

We are susceptible to heretical teachings because, in one form or another, they nurture and reflect the *way we would have it be* rather than the *way God has provided,* which is infinitely better for us. As they lead us into the blind alleys of self-indulgence and escape from life, heresies pander to the most unworthy tendencies of the human heart. It is astonishing how little attention has been given to these two aspects of heresy: its cruelty and its pandering to sin.

The conviction that heresy is cruel has given me a growing awe of and respect for orthodoxy. Unlike many contemporary scholars who seem increasingly to view these classical conciliar statements as irrelevant to the concerns of modern times, or worse, as impediments to be disregarded or obstacles to be overcome, I am convinced that seldom have these guidelines been more relevant than they are today. Neither ignorance of the heresies nor belief in their irrelevance can guard against making the same mistakes. Scarcely any ancient heresy can be found that does not have a modern expression; scarcely is there a modern heresy that we have not seen before.

Some argue that we have now reached a point in education, evolution, democracy, science, and spiritual maturity at which these ancient and classical formularies are rendered irrelevant. On the contrary, it is my conviction that not since the age of the councils have we needed them more urgently. All modern or contemporary attempts to resolve the ancient dilemmas are rarely if ever an improvement on those of Nicaea or Chalcedon. In fact, most of these attempts appear to be only slightly disguised versions of the ancient heresies, and are frequently set forth without any attempt to deal with the original reasons for their rejection.

Any attempt to affirm orthodoxy and criticize heresy goes sharply against the modern trend. Many today firmly regard orthodoxy as dull, unimaginative, defensive, stultifying, and rigid; whereas heresy is bold, imaginative, innovative, and creative. Of course, there is some truth in this view. Defenders of orthodoxy have been at times both dull and cruel. Heretics have sometimes been exceedingly selfless and sincere in their beliefs, often with a tenacious grasp of the partial truth within their teaching while blind to its context or its wider implications.

But the other side is true, too. Some heretics were singularly stubborn, narrow, repressive, and cruel, while many orthodox were courageous, selfless, and magnanimous, often suffering ostracism, exile, and death. Certainly Athanasius, the classic defender of Nicene faith, suffered more for his unpopular orthodox views than did Arius, the "Heresiarch," or "Chief Heretic," for his heretical and popular ones.

The journalistic view of courageous and lonely heretics fighting unequal battles against a well fortified and insensitive orthodoxy is held not only by average persons but even by some scholars. It is now almost shameful to call oneself "orthodox," while the label "heretic" is worn as a badge. Bishop James Pike proudly called his self-defense *If This Be Heresy.* Princeton's Walter Kaufmann titled his personal manifesto *The Faith of a Heretic.* Robert Van de Weyer's *The Call to Heresy* attempts to explain the issues between orthodoxy and heresy on the basis that "the victors write the history" and orthodoxy was simply the version of truth that had the most muscle behind it. This view of heresy versus orthodoxy reflects not so much a concern for truth as an interest in the way groups use power.

The sociologist of religion and culture, Peter Berger, exhorts us all to heresy in *The Heretical Imperative*. This book illustrates well the way in which all self-proclaimed heretics, on close examination, attempt to replace some orthodoxy (right opinion) with their own teaching because they believe theirs is right and therefore orthodox. Cynics who have relinquished any search for truth have claimed that "orthodoxy is what we believe, as heresy is what others believe." Orthodoxy means "right opinion" and right opinion is precisely what everyone believes her or his opinion to be. Successful heretics soon claim their opinion to be "orthodox." Berger's analysis of the current obligation of modern people to make choices about their beliefs is brilliant. He also knows that heresy comes from the word "to choose," so that whether we like it or not there is the "imperative" to choose. Berger's thesis is too important for him to be allowed to clothe himself in today's respectable robes of "heresy" and relegate other Christians to the rags of "orthodoxy."

It is quite clear that Berger advocates an "orthodoxy" in which Rudolph Bultmann is as "wrong" as the church regarded Marcion; Karl Barth is as "wrong" as Arius; and Friedrich Schleiermacher is as "right" as the church held Athanasius to be in the fourth century. Berger is as exclusive toward conservative Evangelicals, Roman Catholics, and Barthians as the historically orthodox have been toward the classical heresies. He is more generous to the beliefs of Hindus and Buddhists than to those of Neo-orthodoxy.

This dynamic by which popularly accepted heresy becomes a new orthodoxy is not confined to Pike, Kaufmann, Van de Weyer, and Berger alone. It is always the case. But we do not lack objective standards to which we can appeal when we disagree about whose doctrine is "correct." Christians have generally used the term "orthodoxy" to mean the creeds and decisions of the first four General (or Ecumenical) Councils of the early church, which have been the accepted guidelines for these many centuries. These statements of the church, which are not so much final solutions as they are limits within which the profound mysteries of the Trinity and the person of Christ should be approached, have come under serious criticism of late, even from within the church.

However, before we disregard them let us look carefully at what is being put in their place. Let us consider the practical and pastoral implications of the old heresies now being dressed up to suit the modern mind. The boundaries that saved the Christian faith from being absorbed into pagan religion and from degenerating into a mere legalistic sect were and are far too valuable to be dismissed, ignored, jettisoned, or hidden away in an academic ghetto.

Whereas successful heresies become new orthodoxies, so also orthodoxy tends to drift into heresy. When the creeds are accepted as correct or orthodox almost immediately orthodox behavior begins to demand assent to the creeds rather than "yes" to the God to whom the creeds point, and thus a new heresy is born from "correct" orthodoxy. This fact can appear to justify all the negative connotations of the word "orthodoxy."

Teachings and ideas have consequences. The fundamental reason for distinguishing between heresy and orthodoxy is the question of truth. The contemporary flight from questions of truth, especially in matters of belief, is disclosed and critiqued by Lesslie Newbigin:

> The relativism which is not willing to speak about truth but only about "what is true for me" is an evasion of the serious business of living. It is the mark of a tragic loss of nerve in our contemporary culture. It is a preliminary symptom of death.[3]

If a teaching is wrong opinion rather than right opinion the consequences are cruel, the Christian faith is distorted, and people who follow these teachings are hurt. Ignoring the pastoral implications of the Councils renders the studies of the Councils virtually irrelevant. But these Councils were then and are now most decisively important to test whether current teachings are wrong (heretical) or right (orthodox).

Bismarck once observed that "war is too serious a matter to be left to the generals." Theology likewise is too serious a matter to be left to the scholars. We cannot do without generals or scholars, but each of us must do our own contending and our own believing. Berger is right about this: we all must choose.

One of the barriers to our choosing the faith of our fathers is the word "orthodoxy." It has a checkered history with a strangely ambivalent and even paradoxical connotation. On the one hand its basic definition has the purest and most positive meaning: *orthos* meaning straight or correct or right or true, and *doxa* meaning opinion and, by extension, teaching. All, including ancient and modern heretics, claim that their teaching or opinion is true and correct. Who would ever claim one's own currently held opinion to be false?

All claims against orthodoxy are made explicitly or implicitly in the name of some new or different orthodoxy. Whether it be communism, modern medicine, Freudianism, or Keynesian economics, the critics or "heretics" always protest in the name of what they perceive to be true and correct doctrine and opinion as oppposed to a conventional, received, or erroneous orthodoxy.

This word "orthodoxy," whose very meaning begs the question of right and true, has somehow attracted to itself unmistakably negative and pejorative connotations such as "not original" or "conventionally approved." "Not independent minded or original" is another meaning found in dictionaries. One must face at the outset the reasons for this development. What makes this issue a matter of crucial concern for Christians is that a justifiable case can be made for the claim that what is conventionally approved has almost always been heresy and not orthodoxy.

21

Another barrier is that orthodoxy, over time, seems to keep its form but lose its substance. This dynamic may be seen as the functional equivalent in the spiritual and institutional world of what physicists call entropy in the physical world. Entropy is that law of physics which shows that in each transaction of mechanical work there is a loss or dissipation of energy.

Similarly, as a fresh wording of Christian truth initially is received with power, over time the expression of that truth begins to be received as the truth itself and its power and energy are dissipated. The creeds are good examples of this dynamic. They are expressions and symbols of the saving action of God. We believe the creeds only in the sense that we believe what they express. The creeds did not hang on a cross for sinners. The human tendency to confuse symbols with what they represent causes the loss of their passion and power, the loss and dissipation of their energy.

This entropy, or dissipation of energy, would seem an apt model to help us understand how orthodoxy tends to lose its power as subsequent generations tend to recite the form without a genuine grasp of its substance. To counter this spiritual entropy and recover the original power of orthodoxy, each generation must struggle anew with its original meaning. It is said of Quakers that "religion gave rise to prosperity and was devoured by its offspring." Similar observations could be made of each tradition, indicating the human tendency to accept the fruit of grace while forgetting its roots.

The Human Factor

The ultimate cruelty of heresy can be shown by approaching the Councils from the concern over what happens to someone who follows teachings outside the limits set by the creeds. A human factor needs to be added to the traditional way in which these Councils are approached. Historical, theological, and philosophical questions are always, and of necessity, diligently treated by studies of these Councils. The question of the fidelity of a given teaching to the data of scripture also is traditionally treated with great rigor. However, the condition of the human heart that receives and conveys the gospel is almost everywhere ignored as a factor in consideration of teachings, whether they be heretical or orthodox.

That the human heart is a "veritable factory of idols" is a truth attributed to various Reformers. The heart is certainly "far gone from original righteousness," and it is a filter through which the gospel must pass in its hearing and its telling. Each heresy in its own way encourages some flaw in our human nature. Without appreciating this human factor one could be led to believe that orthodoxy is a relatively simple matter: the results of proper research and scholarship. The human factor makes us acknowledge that research and scholarship itself must pass through the heart of the researcher and the scholar.

An opposite reaction often appeals to those impatient of the discipline and hard work involved in research and scholarship and whose hearts filter out the tough thought and rigor necessary to mature faith. In either case it is very much this human factor that encourages our idolatry of half-truths, frozen simplicities of childhood, new forms of old heresies, and old forms of orthodoxy without the substance (the spirit) of orthodoxy. The culture's understandably negative reaction to the very term "orthodoxy" reflects this experience in its frequently pejorative use of the term.

Samuel Taylor Coleridge, whose often overlooked theological genius equalled that of his literary accomplishments, once commented on an observation of the seventeenth-century bishop, Jeremy Taylor. "For heresy is not an error of the understanding but an error of the will."[4] Coleridge responded, "Most excellent. To this Taylor should have adhered, and to its converse: Faith is not an accuracy of logic but a rectitude of the heart."[5]

The usually overlooked human factor in the origin of heresy is indeed the will that stems from the human heart. Yet authentic

Christian orthodoxy is a deeper matter than mere correct doctrine, as important as that is. It must be something not less than a "rectitude of the heart."

Some of this material is admittedly difficult and I plead for some patience on the part of the non-specialist reader to wrestle with the issues as Jacob wrestled with the Angel that the reader may similarly be blest in spite of the inadequacy of the presentation. Likewise I plead for patience from the specialist that I may be forgiven for what will doubtless seem to be patronizing to the scholar in my attempt to be as clear and simple as the subject allows. My sincerest hope is that future scholarship on this subject will include a keener sensitivity to the human implication of doctrine. The claim that heresy is largely a matter of sin is a spiritual challenge that begs serious attention.

1

Short Beds and Narrow Blankets

For the bed is too short to stretch oneself on it,
and the covering too narrow to wrap himself in it.
Isa. 28:20

In spite of popular ideas concerning heresies, they are, in fact, narrow and limited ways of understanding Christianity. They are "short beds" and "narrow blankets," but they are inevitable. Any group of Christians today are apt to arrive at conclusions similar to those of the early church as they puzzle over and respond to crucial texts of scripture:

"Why do you call me good? No one is good but God alone." (*Mark 10:18*)

"The Father is greater than I." (*John 14:28*)

Jesus wept. (*John 11:35*)

"I thirst." (*John 19:28*)

And Jesus cried again with a loud voice and yielded up his spirit. (*Matt. 27:50*)

Do these, and other texts like them, mean that Jesus was a good man but not God? Is he merely a human to whom God gave divine attributes? Or was he a remarkable man to whom divine qualities were attributed by disciples and impressionable believers?

Consider, on the other hand, these texts:

"But who do you say that I am?" And Peter answered, "The Christ of God." *(Luke 9:20)*

"He who has seen me has seen the Father." *(John 14:9)*

"I and the Father are one." *(John 10:30)*

In the beginning was the Word and the Word was with God and the Word was God. *(John 1:1)*

He is the image of the invisible God, the first born of every creature. *(Col. 1:15)*

Thomas answered him, "My Lord and my God!" *(John 20:28)*

Do these, and other texts like them, mean that Jesus was indeed God and that God himself took on flesh, suffered and died? Or do they mean that God was in Christ but only appeared to be a man, appeared to suffer, and appeared to die?

Each of these inferences and many more have been made by people reading the Bible or, in the case of the early church, hearing the story of Jesus Christ before it was set down and read as scripture. Misunderstandings and distortions of the gospel message were innumerable, and many of them can be found in one form or another today.

The meaning of these texts must necessarily be asked in each generation and of each individual. "What think ye of Christ?" is a question addressed by our Lord not only to Peter, but to each of us. Christians, in the early centuries, used a three-hundred-year process of accepting and rejecting writings before finally approving certain ones as "canonical" and placing them in what we call the Bible. This process is called "canonizing," and the result is called the "canon of scripture." Over subsequent centuries Christians used a similar process of accepting and rejecting teachings, based on varying responses to questions such as those above, to set limits and boundaries for these teachings. We know these boundaries as our classical creeds.

Personalities, politics, and intrigue were factors in the development of creedal statements. Christianity has never promised its adherents a purely spiritual arena, with wise and selfless leaders working out pure doctrine insulated from and uncontaminated by politics, rivalry, partisanship, fear, strife, and other "works of our fallen nature" *(Gal. 5:19)*. Then as now God has only sinners to do God's work.

After Constantine (318), emperors attempted to use Christianity to bring unity to the empire by coercion, exile, and imprisonment of "heretics." Certainly this imposition and enforcement of the church's teaching by law was one of the less fortunate aspects of the agonizing process of determining orthodoxy.

But the positive aspects of limits on teaching that claimed to be Christian have too often been overlooked in modern times. We fail to appreciate the necessity of preserving Christ's teachings and his work in order to safeguard the graceful and liberating experiences of Christians. As a skull and crossbones on a bottle warns that the contents are poison to our bodies, so the label "heresy" warns us that it is poison to our souls.

One cannot give one's own experience of redemption to another person, much less to another generation. One can only witness to it, describe it, and tell the story of that experience and live in a way that makes the witness believable and attractive. In telling the story, it was then, and is now, crucial to get the story right.

Docetism

One of the earliest versions of the story of Jesus that jeopardized what Christians had experienced was called Docetism. The Docetists found it incomprehensible that Jesus could have actually suffered. They answered the essential questions about him by insisting that he only *appeared* to suffer, to weep, to thirst, to hunger, to sweat in agony, and to die, and that his incarnate human state was so spiritual that he only appeared to be human. (Docetism is derived from the word *dokein,* which means "to seem, to appear.") The faithful denied these teachings early on because telling the story the Docetic way would cause hearers to miss the essential aspects of Christian experience.

Jesus' disciples had known a person who had really been born, had lived through a real childhood, had had a real body, and had experienced real suffering, a real crucifixion, and a real resurrection. His followers in subsequent generations had a similar experience because they had been told the story of a real man and not one who only appeared to be human.

Experiencing and surviving one's own suffering can be one of the transforming realities of a Christian's life. Suffering would have been left untouched, in all its painful and despairing hopelessness, if Docetism, which taught that God in no way has taken on human suffering, had been accepted as authentic Christian teaching.

Too few studies have mentioned the religious and devotional experiences of Christians that led them to reject Docetism. All who had been able to rejoice in their suffering because of its role in the development of patience and hope *(Rom. 5:3, Col. 1:24, James 1:2-4)* insisted passionately that these treasured experiences were dependent upon, and could not be detached from, the experience of Christ's suffering.

The "fellowship of his sufferings" *(Phil. 3:10 AV)* was a key to the new Christian life. We are "heirs of God and fellow heirs with Christ, provided we suffer with him in order that we may also be glorified with him" *(Rom. 8:17).* The apostle Peter reflects the Christian view that turns the experience of suffering wrongly or for righteousness' sake into an occasion to give thanks *(1 Peter 2:19)* and be glad *(1 Peter 3:14).* Such experiences in Christian lives depended upon the thorough repudiation of the Docetic lie.

The Docetic version of Christ's death on the cross was that Simon of Cyrene, who was pressed to help carry Jesus' cross was actually crucified in Christ's stead and thereby saved Christ from the indignity of the crucifixion. Although this version of Christianity was repudiated early, human hope that religion will provide escape from suffering and from the offense that Christ suffered an excruciating execution, has caused it to recur repeatedly in church history, in varied and often more subtle forms.

Islam, which honors Jesus as a great prophet, has adopted and preserved the Docetic teaching about Jesus' escape from suffering on the cross. The shame of crucifixion, which gave power and impetus to Docetism, is hard for twentieth-century minds to comprehend, with our tamed and domesticated familiarity with crucifixes in art and jewelry. The fact that several centuries had elapsed before the crucifix appeared in Christian art testifies to the horror people felt for this form of execution.

> We have grown so used to the idea that the Crucifixion is the supreme symbol of Christianity, that it is a shock to realize how late in the history of Christian art its power was recognized. In the first art of Christianity it hardly appears; and the earliest example, on the doors of Santa Sabina in Rome, is stuck away in a corner, almost out of sight. The simple fact is that the Early Church needed converts, and from this point of view the Crucifixion was not an encouraging subject. So, early Christian art is concerned with miracles, healings, and with hopeful aspects of the faith like the Ascension and the Resurrection. The Santa Sabina Crucifixion is not only obscure but unmoving. The few surviving Crucifixions of the early Church make no attempt to touch our emotions. It was the tenth century, that despised and rejected epoch of European history, that made the Crucifixion into a moving symbol of the Christian faith.[1]

Docetism was influenced by the Greek philosophical notion that a divine being could not suffer, by the hope in some Jewish quarters for a politically victorious Messiah, and by the persistent and understandable human tendency to avoid suffering and to resist any teaching that makes use of it. A contemporary example of Docetic approach to suffering is Christian Science. Mary Baker Eddy taught that the entire material world is unreal, and that suffering is illusory and only appears to exist due to the absence of faith. If one had true and complete faith there would be no pain or suffering (and no death).

As we recall from the introduction, each heresy has some important truth. In a society overdosed on pills, prescriptions, and drugs, and hoping that some mechanical or chemical means may quickly fix pain, the Christian Science "solution" can be attractive to some people. Many physicians are frustrated by patients who do not wish to change a pattern in their lives that is damaging their health. Instead they want the doctor to "give them something for it" that will avoid the need for change. But to the many inevitable cases of real suffering, the Docetic teaching adds an additional burden by making the victim feel guilty for "imagining" real pain.

Docetic detours are far more pervasive in the increasingly popular New Age movement and in the "prosperity gospel" ("come unto us and we shall do thee good"—the promise of fulfillment without suffering). Those following these contemporary religious options recoil as did the ancient Docetists from the "way of the cross," which is so eloquently expressed in William Reed Huntington's prayer:

> Almighty God, whose most dear Son went not up to joy but first he suffered pain, and entered not into glory before he was crucified; Mercifully grant that we, walking in the way of the cross, may find it none other than the way of life and peace; through the same thy Son Jesus Christ our Lord, who liveth and reigneth with thee and the Holy Spirit, one God, for ever and ever. Amen.[2]

The Docetic flight from suffering, so humanly understandable, nevertheless is a way of escape, not a way of the cross. The latter promises not only "life" and "peace," but "fellowship" *(Phil. 3:10 AV)*, "endurance," "character," and "hope" *(Rom. 5:3-4)*. By it we are "heirs with Christ" *(Rom. 8:17)*. Christ's sufferings and ours are the means by which comes our "comfort," the very name of the Holy Spirit *(2 Cor. 1:3-7)*. The essential connection between the Holy Spirit and Christ's and our sufferings can be seen from the fact that *parakaleo* (Paraclete, Comforter) occurs ten times and suffering seven times in these five verses.

The Docetic escape is seductive, indeed, but one that would leave us bereft of true life, peace, fellowship, endurance, character, hope and, most of all, of God's Comforter.

Ebionism

The heresy opposed to Docetism is Ebionism. Its origins are obscure. "Ebion" means poor. It could have originated with someone's name or from our Lord's blessing of the "poor" or from the jibes its critics leveled at it by calling it "poor."

The teaching of the Ebionites, however, has a clear and distinct thrust: they accepted Jesus as Messiah but rejected his divine sonship. He was simply the son of Joseph and Mary upon whom the Spirit of God descended on the occasion of his baptism. This divine sonship was a kind of reward and anointing for having obeyed the law. He thus became the greatest of the prophets but in no way does he release humanity from the burden of the law. On the contrary, he showed that the law can be obeyed by obeying it himself. He was adopted into divinity and became an example to his followers to do likewise.

This view could be called the "Roger Bannister doctrine of the Atonement." Before Roger Bannister no one was able to run a mile in four minutes. Many even declared it physiologically impossible. In breaking the four-minute barrier, however, he broke the psychological impediment in the minds of athletes the world over and scores soon followed him in that accomplishment.

The Ebionites taught that Jesus broke the mental and psychological barrier in the minds of people who felt that righteousness by the law was impossible to win. Jesus had now actually done it and, as a result, he was rewarded with a delegated divinity. The meaning of his life and work was, thus, reduced to an example for us to follow.

The "good news" of this Ebionitic form of Adoptionism is "to try harder." It contains an important truth, as all heresies do, in insisting on the real and actual humanity of Jesus Christ, the necessity "to follow him as Lord," and the inspiration of his example. However, it misses the really good news of "accepting him as Savior," by relegating the meaning of his death to a mere stoic example of how we are to face our death, and it relies on the ability of the human will to fulfill the demands of God.

Adoptionism reduces the essential significance of Jesus Christ to an "example" for his followers to obey. Those who so do will be similarly rewarded with "sonship" and divine acceptance. Adoptionism makes of Christianity a religion of control rather than a religion of redemption and reduces morals to moralism. Christianity becomes a grim striving for a goal never to be reached and is preoccupied with symptoms of sin rather than an attempt to treat the human condition that produces sins. It is always reductionist: it reduces mystery to rationality, unity to a hope for unity, joy to striving, religion to law, and liberty to bondage.

The attraction of Adoptionism stems not only from historical teachings but also from human pride. Anything that flatters our self-sufficiency is apt to be elevated to grounds of pretension which justly evoke the judgment of humor. To illustrate their superiority men often boast about their prowess in sex and procreation. Andrew Jackson, throughout his stormy life, was the object of virulent attempts to insult him on the grounds that he had sired no children. He once replied to his attackers that it was strange indeed that some men took such pride in an endeavor in which "a jackass was their infinite superior."

Adoptionist teaching encourages our self-centeredness. It recurs throughout history because we are self-righteous people who tend to accommodate the gospel to our own righteousness or our hopes for our own righteousness. Yet St. Paul has spoken of himself as being "found in him [Christ], not having a righteousness of my own, based on law, but that which is through faith in Christ, the righteousness from God that depends on faith" *(Phil. 3:9)*.

These Adoptionist teachings, or subtle variations of them, had their particular historical focus in the early church at the see of Antioch, and in spite of early repudiation, Adoptionism continued to appear afresh. In the seventeenth century a new version of it appeared in a teaching called Socinianism, which was based on the heretical views of two sixteenth-century Italian theologians: Fausto and Lelio Socinus. They were opposed by both the Reformers and Roman Catholicism, but their subsequent influence, especially in the Netherlands and in England, has had a lasting detrimental effect, especially in Protestant denominations.

Adoptionism and its later form, Socinianism, picture Jesus as one who was "able not to sin" by the power of his will over the temptations he met. It was an early example of "Christology from below," of a human becoming divine by will power, and it is characterized by exhortation and condemnation of those who fail. The figure of our Lord becomes a "teeth-gritting Jesus" who was able, as we should be, to be righteous. Those of us whose righteousness is inadequate are driven to despair. Those of us whose righteousness needs but some polishing up, and a new try tomorrow, are living in suspended animation. Those of us whose righteousness is sufficient are insufferable.

This Adoptionist twist of the Christian faith can often be discerned as much by the tone as by the teaching. When Jesus met this basic religious posture in the scribes and Pharisees he called them "whitewashed tombs, which outwardly appear beautiful but within they are full of dead men's bones and all uncleanness" *(Matt. 23:27).* No wonder that the adherents of this heresy have been recognizable by their grimness and lack of joy. Christianity is reduced to a religion of law in which everybody fails *(Matt. 5:48)* and Christian hope is reduced to "I'll quit tomorrow." Spiritually, one either despairs in the face of the demands of God or reduces those demands to the level of one's own righteousness. Those who have followed this last way are some of the least becoming figures in the history of the church. The pastoral implications of this heresy is a cruel dynamic of despair or self-righteousness.

Heresy and the Human Will

We are seeing that the human heart is indeed a factory of idols in producing objects other than God for our hope. Bishop Jeremy Taylor in the seventeenth century and Samuel Taylor Coleridge in the nineteenth made essential points concerning the relation between our human will and our heretical teaching. Heresy is largely a "matter of the will" and orthodoxy is not correct logic but a mending of "the heart." The universal thirst for self-righteousness is a significant factor in the recurrence of Adoptionism. Both in its hearing and its telling, the Christian gospel is filtered through a human mind, heart, and spirit whose willfulness tends to deflect and distort the story and its meaning.

The symbiotic relationship between heresy and sin, although largely overlooked in texts on church history, is quite apparent in the development and persistence of Docetism and Adoptionism. The human fear of involvement and the wish to escape are clear elements in the atmosphere in which Docetism flourishes. The human self-centered person always resists the claim of any other center and produces the self-righteousness that twists the gospel into the myriad forms of Ebionism or Adoptionism. In its proclamation and reception the gospel must run the gauntlet of the human will's desire to flee (Docetism) or the struggle to maintain one's self as the center (Adoptionism) as the serpent continues to tempt us that we "will be like gods" (*Gen. 3:5 NEB*).

Either Docetism or Adoptionism

According to the theologian William Porcher DuBose, all heresy can be divided into the two basic types, Docetism or Ebionism. The historian Adolf von Harnack formulated the same helpful division which he termed Pneumatic and Adoptionist. By Adoptionism Harnack meant substantially what DuBose meant by Ebionism. By Pneumatic (from *pneuma:* wind, spirit) he meant the Docetic tendency to deny humanity, flesh, and history for the sake of spirit, unity and the eternal. Docetism found its historical focus and location in the city of Alexandria in Egypt; Adoptionism was associated, as we have seen, with Antioch of Syria.

For our purposes let us use DuBose's Docetism and Harnack's Adoptionism as generalizations from which we can begin to understand not just the definitions of heresies, but something of their inner logic and dynamic. In order to include the factors of the human heart as a filter in both hearing and telling the gospel, we would also be helped by the terms: "flight" and "self-centeredness."

Flight and Self-centeredness

Docetism is the teaching about Christ's spiritual and divine nature that sacrifices his human and historical nature. It grows out of the tendency of fallen human nature to flee risky and vulnerable implications that belong inevitably to the very nature of love, a tendency exemplified by the kind of false spirituality implied in statements such as: "The more I see of people, the more I love God."

Sometimes we speak of our desire to escape administrative and committee tasks for more "spiritual" work when basically we wish to escape listening, patience, and the vulnerability to change (the "incarnational" aspects of love), qualities required in responsible committee tasks. We frequently forget that people are no less human and needy because they are separated from us by doors and walls or by distance. The so-called mundane duties can be every bit as spiritually substantial as those thought to be "religious."

Drugs and suicide are the most dramatic examples of the damaging symbiotic relationship between our fallen nature and the Docetic heresy that lures us away from humanity and history. We use alcohol to feel better by feeling less. It was said in the eighteenth century, "The cheapest way out of Birmingham is a bottle of gin." For "out of Birmingham" one can say "out of this job," "this marriage," or "this life." Human nature's vulnerability to the temptation to escape is shown in the unimaginable expense in money, morals, and cultural corruption that the drug trade costs civilization. A theme that runs through the most popular of Eugene O'Neill's plays (*Mourning Becomes Electra* and *The Iceman Cometh*) is said to be the compulsive use of alcohol, drugs, denial, and fantasy to escape the universal pain of being human. All Docetic heresies thrive on this human tendency to resolve the problems of life by some sort of oblivion, escape, or death.

In contrast to the all too human desire to flee from life and reality, the teaching of Christ's full humanity points us to life and its fullness. "I came that they may have life, and have it abundantly" (*John 10:10*). The poet Robert Frost caught something of this profound courage implicit in Christ's incarnation:

> *But God's own descent*
> *Into flesh was meant*
> *As a demonstration*
> *That the supreme merit*
> *Lay in risking spirit*
> *In substantiation.*[3]

The fully human implication of this "substantiation" was adamantly opposed by the Docetics. Docetism will always appeal to those of us whose commitment to ideals stops when practicing them requires our very presence.

Spirit and ideals are never vulnerable until in some way they are incarnate, made flesh. Christ in his incarnate, earthly life has gone before us into those fearful places of doubt and weakness, enduring even death in order to disclose the Easter victory. This reality of risk and suffering is an inescapable aspect of incarnation and is understandably distasteful, not only in historic Docetism but in all situations of personal immaturity as well.

Love is never risked or expressed until someone loves. Everyone is tempted to love in some way that does not involve risk or responsibility. History provides many examples of people passionately concerned with injustices thousands of miles away but insensitive to and uninvolved in needs closer to home. It is often said of idealists that they are in love with humanity but not with actual people.

A physician once persisted for years in discussing his imminent decision to leave his comfortable life and join Albert Schweitzer's clinic in Africa. He neither went nor did any of the unremunerative tasks other physicians did in the community. It was easier to contemplate one's far-away total commitment and sacrifice than actively to give a few hours of service a week together with other imperfect volunteers amid all the frustrations inevitably associated with committees and organizations. And if indeed he had gone to Africa, would he have altogether escaped the petty jealousies and organizational frustrations he had left at home? The idea of enormous and dramatic sacrifice and service has little value until risked in what Frost termed "substantiation."

"I'm religious but I don't believe in institutional Christianity" is often another Docetic way to say, "I want to be spiritual without any of the ambiguities, frustrations, and responsibilities that embody spiritual commitment." Institutions are embodiments and substantiations of ideals, aims, and values. Docetism is a spiritual abnegation of any responsibility to incarnate ideals, values, or love. It is altogether too easy to love and care in the abstract. Concrete situations of diapers, debts, divorce, or listening to and being with someone in depression and despair, is the test of real love. Docetism is the religious way to escape having love tested in the flesh. All of us are tempted to audit life rather than to participate fully and be tested by it.

Proclaiming the story of Jesus Christ without his full humanity tends to reinforce the human tendency in us all to avoid risk. Docetism is like candy; it tastes good, but eventually it rots the teeth. More fundamental still, the word "risk" is the key: Docetism in all its forms is a religion of flight, of cowardice, of suicide. Docetic heresies grow in the soil of sentimental and antiseptic love where hopes are too small to be disappointing, commitments too shallow for risk, loyalties too slight to be betrayed, passions too weak to be hurt. As we shall see in its more subtle forms, Docetism resolves the problem of being human by the destruction of something human.

There is no vaccination against Docetic temptations, and they become more virulent with the inevitable provocations of institutional corruption and the excuses those provide for us to escape involvement. It has been said that the mission field is "the monasticism of Protestantism," that foreign missions represent to some the idealized "first class" spirituality in Protestant traditions that monasticism has been for Roman Catholics. Some of the keenest wisdom, that discerns the "Docetic factor" in such motivation, is found among screening committees of foreign mission boards and among experienced and wise abbesses and abbots of convents and monasteries. Purists to whom it has not been given "to risk spirit in substantiation" are singularly unsuited for the imperfections and ambiguities of the mission field or of monastic life (or, for that matter, of marrying and of having children).

This Docetism is so seductive that it is universally appealing. Dorothee Sölle of Union Seminary states:

The desire to be in God's image without attaining Christ's image is a desire for immediacy, which wants everything without detour and without self-actualization, a narcissistic desire of the ego to settle down in God, immortal and almighty, that doesn't find it necessary to "let its life be crucified" and to experience the night of pain.[4]

The human tendency to flee the imperfections and vulnerability of actual love is the soil that nurtures Docetism. The Docetic denial of Christ's full humanity and his actual suffering was no mere academic mistake of the mind but the cringing withdrawal of the human spirit from the implications, risks, and responsibilities of incarnate love. But these escapes leave us cruelly bereft of the hope and joy that are discovered only in this involved, incarnate communion of substantiated love.

Adoptionism

As Docetism represents Hellenistic heresies so does Adoptionism represent Judaic heresies. Adoptionism thrives on a quite different set of human impulses from those on which Docetism feeds. The temptation of the serpent to Adam and Eve, "and you will be like gods" *(Gen. 3:5 NEB),* indicates the ancient and perennial human desire to be as god, the center. St. Augustine pointed to this root of disobedience (and of all sin) by insisting that Adam and Eve would not have been tempted to do what God had forbidden

> had not man already begun to seek satisfaction in himself and, consequently, to take pleasure in the words: you shall be as Gods. The promise of these words, however, would much more truly have come to pass if, by obedience, Adam and Eve had kept close to the ultimate and true Source of their being and had not, by pride, imagined that they were themselves the source of their being . . . For whoever seeks to be more than he is becomes less, and while he aspires to be self-sufficing he retires from Him who is truly sufficient for him.[5]

As pride is the root of disobedience, self-centeredness, or the desire to be as gods, is the root of all sin. Stealing is basically an attempt to create a world other than God's in which another person's money, house, spouse, or car is ours. Murder is an attempt to create a world in which our enemy does not exist. All sin stems from the original disobedience rooted in the self-centeredness of pride which seeks to be as gods.

This self-centeredness not only affects one's personal morals and relationships but also infects the heart and will through which we experience the gospel. Adoptionism is the glove that fits the hand of self-centeredness. Reducing the meaning of Christ's atonement merely to an example for us to follow does not necessitate the giving up of self as center. Merely to follow Jesus as our example is called the "exemplary" doctrine which we can easily wear over our unchanged, unrepented, and uncleansed self-centeredness. It is said that "clothes make the man" but such clothes will never make a true man or woman. Yet when we accept Jesus not merely as an example but as our center in a new beginning and a new birth in baptism, we are at the root of our human dilemma and we begin to be transformed. When we die to self and lose ourselves in order to live in Christ as both Lord and Savior we have acknowledged and begun to build upon our true center, which is God. This is the meaning of baptism.

However, just as Docetics resist accepting the substantiation of spirit, so Adoptionists resist giving up self as center and resist that central tenet of the gospel that demands a new center, a new birth. Some of the dynamics of Adoptionism can be seen in the Judaizing party that is condemned in the Epistle to the Galatians. The Judaizers taught that the benefits of Christ were attained by a righteousness that is ours because we have obeyed the law, rather than by a righteousness of Christ that we receive by trust (faith) in him. Adoptionists have carefully taken scriptural texts out of context in order to justify their teaching:

Unless your righteousness exceeds that of the Pharisees, you will never enter the kingdom of heaven. *(Matt. 5:20)*

He who does right is righteous. *(1 John 3:7)*

But be doers of the word, and not hearers only. *(James 1:22)*

You see that a man is justified by works and not by faith only. *(James 2:24)*

For Adoptionists the description of Jesus' baptism has been crucial:

> . . . and behold, the heavens were opened and he saw the Spirit of God descending like a dove, and alighting on him; and lo, a voice from heaven, saying, "This is my beloved Son, with whom I am well pleased." *(Matt. 3:16-17)*

This text indicates to them that Jesus' baptism was a kind of knighting ceremony in which some measure of divinity was conferred upon him as a result of God's being "well pleased" with him. As we have seen, Jesus thus becomes the example for all to follow. He is not a new Adam but a new Moses. Adoptionists would have us strive to fulfill the law as set out by Jesus' life. They never seem to understand that it is not that we have *got* to love, but that we *get* to love. Jesus does not call us to a grim attempt to attain; he offers us a joyful opportunity to respond.

This view of Jesus fulfilling the law and consequently being adopted and delegated with divinity leaves out that prior initiative of God:

> . . . while we were yet sinners Christ died for us. *(Rom. 5:8)*

> . . . not that we loved God but that He loved us. *(1 John 4:10)*

In the beginning was the Word. . . *(John 1:1)*

Adoptionism lacks that prophetic preparation and anticipation seen in the Old Testament and seeks not a messiah but a new Moses. It fails to comprehend the necessity and impossibility of perfect human righteousness. Confident (or compulsive) in his own attempt to keep self as center, the Adoptionist sees no reason to avail himself of the God-given perfect righteousness in Jesus Christ that begins to make sinners righteous.

The Adoptionist's concept of righteousness is static rather than dynamic, passive rather than active. If one were to say that a particular homemaker is clean, one might assume she had nothing to do with dirt, whereas in reality what is meant by being a clean homemaker is that she cleans up the dirt. Hence, God is not merely "of purer eyes than to behold iniquity" but also the "God and Father of our Lord Jesus Christ" who enters, dwells in, cleans and redeems us from iniquity. The divine justice is not a passive but an active characteristic by which God makes the unjust just. Thus, the new covenant provides the context for sinners to see themselves, though condemned by the law, as objects of Christ's righteousness by which they are cleansed and redeemed.

Adoptionists believe in the law as having the power to redeem and thus they are unable to make sense of Paul's claim "the sting of death is sin and the power of sin is the law" (1 Cor. 15:56). Even though the law is "holy and just and good" (Rom. 7:12), it does not have the power to break the bondage of sin. It even gives power to sin: ". . . but when the commandment came, sin revived and I died; the very commandment which promised life proved to be death to me" (Rom. 7:9-10). The law can convict, diagnose, inhibit, and sometimes, for a while, control, but it cannot redeem. As Docetism is a religion of escape and not of fulfillment, so Adoptionism is a religion of control, not of redemption.

Another notoriously difficult text for Adoptionists is the comforting one, "Take my yoke upon you, and learn from me; for I am gentle and lowly in heart, and you will find rest for your souls. For my yoke is easy, and my burden is light" (Matt. 11:29-30). How can this be reconciled with the stringent picture of righteousness in the Sermon on the Mount in which Jesus proclaimed, ". . . unless your righteousness exceeds that of the scribes and Pharisees you will never enter the kingdom of heaven" *(Matt. 5:20)* and "You, therefore, must be perfect, as your heavenly Father is perfect" *(Matt. 5:48)*?

If Christianity is but law and example how can the yoke be light in the face of that vision of the kingdom given in Chapters 5, 6, and 7 of Matthew's Gospel? Only with a gospel of grace is it possible to have an easy yoke and its fruit of love, joy, and peace.

"Christ hath brought the market down" are the words of Henry Hammond, a seventeenth century divine, who follows an Adoptionist tradition. By this he meant that the demands of the New Covenant were lowered and not as exacting as those in the Old Covenant. One wonders how he could thus interpret the Sermon on the Mount. Adoptionists then and now give tortuous interpretations of chapters 5 to 7 of Matthew, seeking to lower the demands of our Lord's kingdom to a level they themselves can fulfill. They fail to understand the Sermon on the Mount as a preparation for, and an introduction to, Good Friday, so that, having seen the hopelessness of salvation by our own righteousness we empty ourselves before the crucified Lord. Accepting God's gift of salvation, and relinqishing the vain hope of the sufficiency of our own righteousness, is the easy yoke, the light burden.

The modern Adoptionist squirms before the Sermon on the Mount and insists that "Ye, therefore, must be perfect" does not really mean "perfect." Although the meaning of the word (*teleioi*) translated "perfect," also means "to fulfill," those commentators, seeking to relieve us of judgment, forget that the same word in the same verse is used to describe God. To postulate a lesser demand for the meaning of perfect is to proclaim a lesser god. Adoptionists have missed not only the humor but the whole point of the rich man's difficulty in getting into the kingdom of heaven, harder than a "camel to go through the eye of a needle" *(Mark 10:25)*. They insist that there was in Jerusalem a gate, called the "needle gate," which was too narrow for a camel to pass through easily. Such Adoptionists are aptly called "camel squeezers." They teach that it is not impossible, only very difficult, for a rich man, like a burdened camel, to be squeezed into the kingdom.

If this were a proper interpretation, it would make the rest of the story meaningless. The disciples then asked Jesus, "Who can be saved?" Jesus looked at them and said, "For mortals it is impossible, but not for God; for God all things are possible" *(Mark 10:26,27 NRSV)*.

Theodotus the Tanner, a second-century Adoptionist, taught that Jesus was a "mere man" who received the Spirit of God in a special way at his baptism. Following him, Paul of Samosata, a third-century metropolitan of Antioch, insisted that "wisdom dwelt in him as in no others," meaning, in degree but not in kind, that Jesus was just more of what all people are as divine sons. For Paul of Samosata "the deity grew by gradual progress out of humanity."[6] The primary concerns of the Antiochene approach are righteousness, law, history, and ethics. God has given humanity a covenant in which the individual is responsible to fulfill his or her part. Jesus has shown that it could be done and is an example for us to follow.

We have learned from DuBose and Harnack that all heresies can loosely be seen as either Docetic or Adoptionist. These two ways of distorting the Gospel were present at the very earliest time and, because they each reflect the tendencies of human nature to flee or to establish its own self-centeredness, they were given impetus then and continue to occur in church history.

The great Anglican evangelist Canon Bryan Green used as a theme in all of his missions the song, "Cast your eyes upon Jesus, look full in his wonderful face, for the things of earth shall grow strangely dim in the light of his Glory and Grace." While visiting Virginia Theological Seminary, he told his congregation that he quit using that song because he had been persuaded that it was Docetic.

Things do not grow dim in the light of Christ. They become

clearer and more distinct. One sees the hungry and needy one never noticed before. One sees one's family, enemies, friends, and nature more clearly and in a new light, not more dimly. One does not need to be too exact about what the song means to everyone who sings it, but Canon Green is right to avoid a possible interpretation that is an ancient and perennial distortion of Christian faith.

On the other hand, out of the Adoptionist stable runs this unfortunately popular donkey of a song: "Give me your unconditional love, the kind of love I deserve." Of all themes in the New Testament, none is more prominent than that the love God gives us is *not* the love we deserve but an unearned, unmerited, and undeserved love. The combination of Adoptionist heresies with the self-indulgence of the "Me" generation produces people devoid of the grace of self-sacrifice and self-surrender. When anything is gotten because it is deserved, there are no thanks, no gratitude, no joy, for joy is the fruit of gratitude. When God's love becomes an entitlement and not a gift, the self needs no repentance, no change, and it remains in the cruel and tragic isolation and self-centeredness that we have seen to be the human dynamic in Adoptionist heresies. A New York professional actor and musician says that God has given him the gift of song and he will continue to spread the word that "God will be whatever you want him to be."[7]

Fortunately, however, there are counterforces that help correct these heresies. In its quite different way, each heresy denies such a measure of gospel truth that what is left is unable to produce in its adherents enough change, life, and love to evoke many permanent followers. Thus heresy tends in the long run to die of its own error. As reality itself is the great enemy of a lie so the fruits by which "you will know them"*(Matt. 7:16)* is in the long run the best test of true doctrine. To put it positively, orthodoxy defeats these heresies because it does not pander to human cowardice by encouraging flights from life and history; it provides for its followers something of the promised experience: "I came that they might have life, and have it abundantly" (*John 10:10*). Neither does orthodoxy encourage human self-centeredness, and its followers experience a real measure of joy in the discovery that "whoever loses his life for my sake will save it" (*Luke 9:24*).

Although it is true that heresy tends to burn itself out as it is tested in reality, the same can be said of a fire in one's house. Heresy needs to be corrected before unnecessary and preventable harm is done. Fortunately for the early church, there were some eloquent defenders of the faith.

One such defender was Melito, Bishop of Sardis. Little was known of his second-century writings until some of them were recovered in 1940 (he died ca. 190). The following excerpts from his sermon "Concerning the Passover" show the clear and eloquent affirmation denied by contemporary and modern Docetics and Adoptionists.

> The mystery of the Lord is both new and old, old inasfar as it is prefiguration, new inasfar as it is grace. But if you gaze steadily upon this prefiguration, you will see the reality by way of its fulfillment.
>
> So if you want to see the mystery of the Lord, gaze upon Abel who was similarly murdered, Isaac who was similarly bound. Joseph who was similarly sold for slavery, Moses who was similarly exposed, David who was similarly persecuted, the prophets who similarly suffered on account of the Christ. Gaze also upon the sheep sacrificed in the land of Egypt and the one who smote Egypt and saved Israel by means of blood. . .
>
> He arrived on earth from the heavens for the sake of the one who suffered. He clothed himself in the sufferer by means of a virgin's womb and came forth as a human being. He took to himself the sufferings of the sufferer by means of a body capable of suffering, and he destroyed the sufferings of the flesh. By a Spirit incapable of death he killed off death, the homicide. . .
>
> The Lord, when he had put on the human being and suffered for the sake of him who suffered and was bound for the sake of

him who was imprisoned and was judged for the sake of the condemned and was buried for the sake of the bound, rose from the dead and cried aloud, "Who will enter into judgment against me? Let him stand up and face me. I have set the condemned free. I have given the dead life. I have raised up the one who was entombed. Who will speak against me? I," he says, "the Christ, I have dissolved death. I have triumphed over the enemy and trodden down Hades and bound the strong man and carried off humanity into the height of the heavens—I," he says, "the Christ."

This is he who made the heavens and the earth, and formed humanity in the beginning, who is announced by the Law and the Prophets, who was enfleshed in a Virgin, who was hanged on the Tree, who was buried in the earth, who was raised from the dead and went up into the heights of heaven, who is sitting on the right hand of the Father, who has the authority to judge and save all things, through whom the father made the things which exist, from the beginning to all the ages. This one is "the Alpha and the Omega," this one is "the beginning and the end" the beginning which cannot be explained and the end which cannot be grasped. This one is the Christ. This one is the King. This one is Jesus. This one is the Leader. This one is the Lord. This one is he who has risen from the dead. This one is he who sits on the right hand of the Father. He bears the Father and is borne by the Father. "To him be the glory and the power to the ends of the ages. Amen." [8]

2

Attacks on Christian Faith

Fere libenter homines quod volunt credunt
(People willingly believe what they wish)
Julius Caesar[1]

As the story of the good news spread into the Mediterranean world, a variety of misrepresentations of and omissions from the gospel occurred. The church quite early found it necessary to set limits and to correct teachings that threatened the Christian experience, contradicted the gospel and fed on the human temptations to flight and self-centeredness. These limits are called creeds.

Obviously Jesus did not go around with a blackboard with the creeds written on it, letting his disciples ask questions and explaining the meaning of his relationship with the Father and the Holy Spirit as well as the relationship between his divinity and his humanity. He did not ask the disciples for assent to propositions about himself. The creeds were only gradually developed to distinguish the Christian faith from Docetic and Adoptionist twists. Those who attempted to take the faith into either of these two directions were called heretics (from *haireo* - to choose) who chose for themselves an interpretation contrary to that received by the faithful whose lives had been radically changed.

Heretics actually made a contribution to this process by forcing the Christian Church both to set some limits on what could properly be called "Christian" and to preserve the essentials of the story of Jesus Christ so that the faithful would not be led into the destructive directions of flight or self-centeredness. One person who served this function in the second century was Marcion.

Marcion was born about 85 in Sinope on the shores of the Black Sea in what is now modern Turkey. He was the son of a bishop and had made quite a fortune in sea trade. He taught for a while in Asia Minor but was excommunicated by his own father for his teachings. (Were a twentieth century bias operative in the second century, with personal relationships accorded higher value than questions of truth, the bishop would probably be excoriated and Marcion made a popular "cutting edge" hero.) Marcion came to Rome about 139 and was initially well received, due to his brilliance and generosity to the church. But when he presented his ideas and theology to the church in Rome, they, too, excommunicated him (and, commendably, returned his money).

His views, which were condemned, were:

1. The God of the Old Testament, the lawgiver demanding righteousness, was evil. The God of the New Testament is a different God, one who is good and merciful.

2. The creator was evil.

3. Christ was divine; he only appeared to be human.

4. The Old Testament was rejected and only Paul's epistles and portions of St. Luke's Gospel were accepted.

5. Some statements in Paul's epistles, which referred positively to the Old Testament or to the goodness of the law, were suppressed.

6. Grace is the opposite of law; love is the opposite of justice. God and good people are unable to punish.

In the second century there was no written New Testament as we know it today. Certain books were generally accepted quite early as "scripture." Only after a slow and lengthy process, greatly stimulated by the reaction to Marcion, were the twenty-seven books we now have as New Testament finally pronounced as canonical in the fourth century.

Marcion founded his own church and his ideas spread rapidly throughout the empire, especially in Greek regions where Neoplatonic philosophy was more conducive to Docetism, and where anti-Semitism could be counted on to repudiate the Jewish roots of Christianity. We are made aware of the enormous influence of Marcion by the number of early church fathers who felt it necessary to write against his teaching: Justin, Irenaeus, Tertullian, Hippolytus, and Epiphanius.

Irenaeus

Irenaeus (ca. 130-ca. 200) was the greatest of these early theologians and was among the first to focus, not on the presentation of Christianity to pagans, but on the misrepresentations of Christianity among Christians. His chief book is called *Against Heresies,* and to him much of the credit must be given for preserving Christian teaching from the distortions of Marcion and others.

A contemporary of Marcion and Irenaeus, whose misguided ministry flourished in the second half of the second century, was Montanus. As Marcion had cut off the Old Testament and most of the New, Montanus added his own revelation and those of other ecstatic and charismatic prophets.

Claiming to be the incarnation of the Holy Spirit as Jesus had been of the logos, Montanus gathered together large numbers of people dedicated to the strictest asceticism and practice of ecstasy to await the promised Second Coming. The teaching of Irenaeus concerning scripture did more than anything else to give the church the means to deal with these excesses. Written sources of scripture, Irenaeus insisted, were the sole ultimate criterion of authority in Christian teaching.

Thus the church preserved the Old Testament and those New Testament writings that differed from the beliefs of Marcion, while, at the same time, the church fathers denied the Montanist and cultic claims of new revelations that superceded that given in Christ. Irenaeus's confidence that a full and not incomplete (as Montanus claimed) saving revelation was given in Christ saved the church from subtracting from that revelation, as Marcion would have it, and from adding to that revelation the cultic presumptions of Montanus.

The enormous contribution of Irenaeus is difficult to appreciate from the viewpoint of subsequent centuries. Marcion's brilliance and talents had evoked a large following of people who were only too willing to follow a distortion of Christianity that promised escape from law and entanglements of "this wicked world." Likewise, the claims of Montanus to new and special revelations and self-embodiments of the Holy Spirit were so popular that some towns in Asia were abandoned by almost every Christian, as they gave up spouses and property and followed Montanus in setting up a new city to await the Second Coming. Scarcely a century goes by without several unfortunate examples of new expressions of the ideas of Marcion and Montanus.

In his day Irenaeus had the backing of neither an official canon of scripture nor of an official creed. The Apostles' Creed was generally known but had as yet no official standing and was not explicit enough to meet the heretical teachings of the second century. *Against Heresies* was thus especially important in distinguishing the true nature of Christianity from these gross distortions.

Recapitulation is the main concept in Irenaeus's theology. By this he meant the renewal of creation, not its destruction. God himself created humanity and the world, the world being good and humankind made in the image and likeness of God. The fall had distorted both creation and human nature, so that both were without hope except by God's action in Christ.

"As in Adam all die, even so in Christ shall all be made alive" *(1 Cor. 15:22).* This was a pivotal text for Irenaeus's view of salvation by recapitulation: Jesus traversed the same ground as Adam, but by obedience rather than disobedience. Jesus experienced each stage of human development—infancy, childhood, youth, and mature adulthood—sanctifying each by obedience *(cf. Hebrews 5:8,9),* as Adam, by his disobedience, had lost for us the likeness of God, the remaining "image" being disordered by sin and death. This loss of human "likeness" to God, and the distorted "image" of God remaining in our nature, is the source of our woundedness that reminds us of a lost glory but, at the same time, exceeds all nature in the resulting human capacity for depravity. The "recapitulation" of Christ's obedience redeems us from this fallen human condition.

The often overlooked contribution of Irenaeus was this affirmation of the essential role of Christ's humanity. Although Marcion and Montanus appear to be opposite in their respective subtraction and addition to the revelation of Christ, they are one in the Docetic and Gnostic category in denigrating the full humanity of Christ. Irenaeus's firm insistence upon the fullness of Christ's humanity helped save Christianity from being absorbed into a culturally larger Gnostic system (discussed below), which taught and promised escape rather than redemption.

Some modern admirers of Irenaeus have seized upon his "creation" doctrine to substitute it for the "redemptive" motif in Christianity. This is to misunderstand Irenaeus completely. His re-creation is redemption as Christ undoes for us what was otherwise the irredeemable condition of human life since Adam's disobedience.

The recapitulation by Christ's obedience was not a form of Adoptionism but the very task that the logos took on in the Incarnation. Christ was one of the "hands" of God by which we are brought into our lost "likeness." The Holy Spirit is the other "hand" of God by which we are brought to Christ and through Christ to God.

The key to Irenaeus's teaching is its soteriological (study of salvation) focus: the purpose of Christianity is salvation, the restoration of humans to unity with God. All philosophical and religious speculation is merged into the single concern of scripture's story of salvation. Irenaeus does not speculate on the relationships between the Father, Son, and Holy Spirit but contents himself with describing their functions in the saving of humankind. His is one of the earliest theological expressions of the doctrine of the Trinity.

Two crucial affirmations mark the lasting contribution of Irenaeus. First, "The Son of God (has) become a son of man"; that is, the redemptive work of Christ depends fully on the identity of his humanity with our humanity. Second, "Jesus Christ, [is] true man and true God." Our salvation depends upon the fact that "God was in Christ, reconciling the world unto himself" *(2 Cor. 5:19)*. This high point of theology concerning Christ and his work (Christology) was not to be attained again until the Council of Chalcedon three centuries later.

To summarize Irenaeus's message: Christ's person and work was to reunite God and humanity, to undo Adam's disobedience and defeat by his obedience and victory, and so restore to humanity both the image and likeness of God. This necessitates the giving of the Spirit which

> descended from God on the Son of God, made Son of man, and with him became accustomed to dwell among the human race, and to rest on man, and to dwell in God's creatures, working the Father's will in them, and renewing them from their old state into the newness of Christ.[2]

> Already we receive some portions of his Spirit for our perfecting and our preparation for immortality, as we gradually become accustomed to receive and bear God. This is what the apostle calls a "first instalment" . . . and makes us even now spiritual . . . not by getting rid of the material body, but by sharing in the Spirit. . . . If because we have the first instalment we cry, "Abba! Father", what will happen when on rising we see him face to

face? . . . the whole grace of the Spirit . . . will make us like him and will perfect in us the Father's will, for it will make man in the image and likeness of God.[3]

Gnosticism

Irenaeus' magisterial contribution was not limited to his check on Marcionism and Montanism; he also took on the wider, more pervasive and more difficult to define phenomenon, Gnosticism. Gnosticism (from the Greek word for knowledge, *gnosis*) is a term embracing many heresies that share certain attributes and characteristics. This exceedingly influential way of religious thinking is becoming the most prevalent category of heresies in modern times.

The early church fathers, the study of whom we call Patristics, are virtually unanimous in seeing Simon Magus, who offered money for the spiritual power he saw in the apostles *(Acts 8:18,19)*, as the father or forerunner of Gnosticism. For Gnostics, salvation is by knowledge *(gnosis)*. Gnosticism, then and now, is characterized by claims to special knowledge held by an intellectual elite who are on their way to becoming super-spirits. In the early versions that Irenaeus encountered there were many gods, but the supreme one was unknowable. From this supreme god came a descending hierarchy of lesser gods called "emanations" or "aeons." According to one Basilides (died ca. 140) of Egypt, there were 365 heavens. The ruler of the angels who made the lowest heaven was the God of the Jews and was evil. Thus, creation was evil. Furthermore, Christ only appeared to be a man. Simon of Cyrene was crucified in Christ's place, while Christ returned to the supreme God. Salvation provided an escape from the evil conditions of fleshly existence by knowledge of the secret incantations by which one could climb through the 365 heavens.

The "species" of Gnosticism vary from the Gnosticism of an unknowable god to a Gnosticism regarding a pure human nature imprisoned in a corrupt body. Marcion shared many of the Gnostic tenets, except in his insistence that salvation is by faith rather than by knowledge. We can also see that Docetism is a form of Gnosticism. Docetism is the "Christological Gnosticism" which denies the fullness of Christ's human nature and the reality of his suffering.

The characteristics of Gnosticism can be generally summarized by its teaching of a supreme unknowable God among many gods, a dualism between spirit (good) and body (bad), the necessity of a secret (esoteric) knowledge in order to be saved, and evil being located in the order of nature. Gnosticism attempted to absorb and accommodate Judaism and Christianity into its system. It represented a serious threat to the Christian church, and, if it had succeeded, Christianity would have become a very different religion, one characterized by escape.

Irenaeus' work not only set out the clear scriptural teachings against the attempt by Gnostics to distort and absorb Christianity, but he did so with humor. He lampoons the Gnostic system of Valentinus in a satire in which the supreme god, "Only Begotten," produces another spiritual aeon, "Utternothingness," which in turn produces an aeon called "Gourd" which is palpable, edible, and delicious. "Gourd" in turn produces "Cucumber," and these four then generate all the other "delicious melons of Valentinus."[4]

The "elitism" of Gnosticism, in which only a few are "in the know" and able to understand and receive knowledge necessary for salvation, appeals to "superior" intellects in each age. The intoxication of being one of the few to possess the secret, saving knowledge, together with the prospect of being freed from the frustrations of bodily existence, has much of the same appeal that drugs possess—escape. The insistent theme of orthodoxy, that humanity needs redemption from the effects of its distorted and sometimes evil will rather than from the effects of an evil environment, is not nearly as appealing or seductive to the immature as the hope of escape by a change in venue, job, spouse, house—or religious itinerary.

Because of the radical dualism that regarded the flesh or body as the source of evil, Gnosticism can be either very ascetical or very licentious. Creation of woman was regarded by some Gnostics as the origin of evil, and procreation of children was but the multiplication of souls in bodily bondage to powers of darkness. Certain "Pneumatics" (spiritual ones), though encapsulated in flesh, have sparks of the divine and, being "pearls," cannot be sullied by external mud; they are therefore immune spiritually to whatever happens in their bodies. Here is justification for either extreme ascetical practice or sexual license. The former can demonstrate one's contempt for, and freedom from, the source of evil (the body); the latter can show that the spirit is not contaminated by what the body does. Scarcely a generation goes by without some recurrence of these old heresies. (See Chapter 10 for some contemporary examples.)

Hunger for the inside, secret, esoteric knowledge possessed by the elite alone is fed by very selective use of scripture. Jesus preached that "they may hear but not understand" *(Mark 4:12)* but to the twelve he said, "to you has been given the secret of the kingdom of God, but for those outside, everything is in parables" *(Mark 4:11)*. Then Jesus took only three of the twelve, Peter, James, and John, to show them even more inner secrets on the Mount of Transfiguration *(Matt. 17:1* and *Mark 9:2)*.

The desire for secrets of inside knowledge and elitism are aspects of human nature that will always make Gnosticism appealing. One seminary professor advised his younger colleagues, "You're wasting your time with 85 percent of the class. You might as well concentrate on the 15 percent who have the intelligence to understand." This elitism is characteristic of Gnosticism and remains a prominent factor in the notorious pedagogical ineptness of some brilliant scholars. When academic language becomes so unnecessarily arcane that scholars speak only to scholars, the nonscholarly student is apt to respond in sullen retreat from the necessary rigor of legitimate study. It is always salutary to recall that "not many of you were wise according to worldly standards . . . but God chose what is foolish in the world to shame the wise" (cf. 1 Cor. 1:26-32). This is an excellent anti-Gnostic counter to the persistent temptation to make Christianity a subject for the elite alone. In fact, the Gnostic tendency of the Corinthian church was the main target of Paul's letter. The entire first Epistle is a timeless response to the perennial conditions that arise in churches through the ages.

One of the spiritual hazards of scholarship is that it can become Gnostic. A lifetime of submersion in conceptual and subtle complexities with an ever more sophisticated vocabulary can seduce some of the best scholars into elitism, inept pedagogy, and irrelevance. I recall listening to the Washington Redskins being defeated by the Los Angeles Raiders by the score of 35 to 9. The announcer asked, "What is Theisman going to do now? Will he call a draw play or will he pass? Well, there are only seven seconds left to play so it's all academic now!" It was the first time that I had noticed that "academic" had come to mean "irrelevant" or "it doesn't matter." This unfortunate development has been brought about largely by Gnostic elitism and scholars' failure to relate their work to the real world.

Another important aspect in the dynamic that undergirds Gnosticism and Docetism is the denigration or scapegoating of the body. A young man who slept through an agreed 6 a.m. date to go jogging had as his excuse, "The spirit was willing but the flesh was weak." "You lie!" came the not unfriendly reply, "Don't blame your flesh. It was not your flesh but your spirit. Your spirit told your hand to shut off the alarm on the clock and turned your body over to go back to the sleep your will desired. Don't try to make your body the scapegoat for the responsibilities your spirit deserves!" Too few friendships are marked by such theologically precise candor. True, his excuse was a text from the mouth of Jesus but only rarely does this accurately describe our actions.

Instead, we all tend to make scapegoats of our bodies. The scripture tells us that "no one hates his own flesh" (Eph. 5:29).

As a generalization and as an ideal this is true. Unfortunately there are persistent incidents of the ideal being disastrously violated. People have too frequently mutilated their bodies in a perverse desire to "make amends" or "make restitution" for some sense of guilt. A great deal of modern sickness is the result of destructive neglect or abuse of one's body, making it into a scapegoat. "He worked himself to death" is sometimes spoken as if it were a virtue, which it could be in a Gnostic religion.

In his book *Principles of Self-Damage*, a modern psychiatrist, Edmund Bergler, spells out in clinical detail this human dynamic of self-sabotage and self-damage that is alarmingly pervasive and not at all relegated to those perceived as masochists. This dynamic leaves us with a thirst for distortions of the Gospel that tempt us to resolve the problems of earthly existence by a self-sabotaging escape from flesh and time. Gnostic versions of Christianity saw both flesh and time as prisons for our alledgedly pure and innocent souls.

The persistence of this idea through the centuries is indicated by Robert Browning's nineteenth-century poem, "Paracelsus":

> *Truth is within ourselves: it takes no rise*
> *From outward things, whatever you may believe.*
> *There is an inmost center in us all,*
> *Where truth abides in fullness; and around,*
> *Wall upon wall, the gross flesh hems it in,*
> *This perfect, clear perception—which is truth.*
> *A baffling and perverting carnal mesh*
> *Binds it, and makes all error: and to know*
> *Rather consists in opening a way*
> *Whence the imprisoned splendor may escape,*
> *Than in effecting entry for a light*
> *Supposed to be without.*

This was favorably quoted in, of all places, a church bulletin. While discussing its radical distortion of Christianity, a young woman responded, "I see nothing wrong with that. Isn't that the way things are?" This same young woman later committed suicide and in such a way as to show she meant to free the "truth" and "light" of her "inmost center" by a dreadful attack with a knife on her "gross flesh." Life and suicide are always far more complex than we can understand, but whatever self-damaging dynamic was part of her tragic death, it was not helped by the heretical teaching she had unfortunately absorbed from within the church.

The teaching in this poem can be found nowhere in the Old or New Testaments. It is diametrically opposed to the prologue to John's Gospel, and is mercifully absent from the *Book of Common Prayer* used by Browning in the nineteenth and this woman in the twentieth century. It has been taught as heretical by every branch of Christianity. How can it occur again except that it appeals to some unfortunate self-damaging longing in the human heart?

Another factor that fuels this self-sabotaging human dynamic and makes Docetic and Gnostic heresies appealing to many of us is the misunderstanding of the word in the New Testament translated "flesh." *Sarx* is used by St. Paul to mean that "lower nature" or self-destructive dynamic in unredeemed human nature that produces what are called in Galatians 5 the "works of the flesh." Some of these we would understand today to be of the flesh: fornication, impurity, and licentiousness. However, most of those works are nothing like what a person today would call flesh: idolatry, sorcery, enmity, strife, jealousy, anger, selfishness, dissention, and so forth.

What St. Paul means by "flesh" is that aspect of unredeemed human nature which gives rise to corruption and destruction. Our *nature,* not our *bodies,* produces the fleshly works of envy, strife, and so forth. Flesh is not to be contrasted with soul. In the New Testament, works of the soul are shown to be as destructive as works of the flesh. *Sarkikos* (fleshly) and *psukikos* (from the word for "soul") are virtually synonymous and interchangeable. Both are used in contrast to *pnuematikos* (spiritual). The latter, however, does not describe the spirit of *natural* humanity but of human nature led by the Holy Spirit, thus producing the "fruit of the Spirit": love, joy, peace, patience, kindness, goodness, faithfulness, gentleness, self-control.

The importance of this brief discussion of these words lies in the fact that scripture was, and continues to be, understood to mean precisely what St. Paul was *not* saying. Our bodies are not evil while our souls are good. Both bodies and souls are in need of redemption. It is a vain and cruel hope that we would be wholesomely spiritual if our souls were not imprisoned in flesh. On the contrary, our fallen nature expresses itself not just in our bodies but in our souls. Love, joy, peace, and so forth are the fruit not of our souls, which are as self-centered as our bodies, but of the Holy Spirit.

Because of awkward problems of translation, the contrast in Galations 5 between flesh and spirit has encouraged countless generations to make scapegoats of their bodies. (*Soma,* the word for "body," is never used in scripture as the origin of sin.) Recognizing this crucially important difficulty, scarcely any translators in this century continue to use the word "flesh" to translate *sarx.* Instead they attempt to get to its New Testament meaning by such terms as "sinful nature" (*New International Version*), "lower nature" (*New English Bible*), "human nature" (*Good News For Modern Man*), and "self-indulgence" (*New Jerusalem Bible*). Only the *Revised Standard Version* still follows the *King James* in using the English word "flesh." (Goodspeed's "physical nature" is inexcusable and an example of the tenacity of Gnosticism in the bosom of scholarship.)

One of the most virulent of early Gnostic heresies made use of these misunderstandings of scripture and flourished in the soil of the human temptation to make our bodies scapegoats and to attribute the origin of evil to the material world.

Manichaeism

Manichaeism is a form of Gnosticism. More than a heresy,

Manichaeism was a well-organized religion with aspects that predate Christianity. It spread from Persia westward through Egypt, North Africa, Rome, and Southern Europe. Eastward it penetrated through India and into China. Its founder, Mani (216 - 274), was born near the site of Baghdad and had a vision in which he saw himself as the successor to Zoroaster, Buddha, and Jesus. He called himself the Paraclete. He was deeply influenced by Gnosticism with its ultimate dualism between light and darkness. He taught that humans were caught in a material world that is neither light nor dark but a "smudge" (Professor F. C. Burkitt's word). Although the teaching did not wholly equate spirit with good or matter with evil, this was the prevailing emphasis.

Adherents were divided between the elect or perfect and hearers or auditors, a typically Gnostic distinction. The former repudiated darkness by leading lives of celibacy and austerity, teaching and preaching. They were served by the hearers who were laypeople. The latter might marry once, but all sensual pleasures were forbidden and the begetting of children was discouraged. The elect were assured of immediate felicity after death. The hearers hoped to be reborn as the elect. All others were doomed to hell.

St. Augustine was himself a Manichaean hearer for nine years before his conversion to Christianity. Elements of Manichaeism can be traced from the third century through the Paulicians in the eastern Mediterranean, to the Bogomiles in the Balkans, to the Albigensians (or Cathari) in southern France who flourished during the eleventh and twelfth centuries. The latter were Docetic concerning Christ and were divided between "the Perfect" and "the Believers," who corresponded to the Manichaean "elect" and "hearers." They contrasted the Latin word for love, *amor*, with the Latin word *roma*, thereby claiming that the Church of Rome had reversed not only the letters but the true content of love. Albigensians were extremely ascetic, bound to absolute chastity and obliged to abstain from eating flesh in all its forms, including eggs, milk, and cheese, which were products of sexual intercourse. Suicide by starvation was a commendable escape from an evil world and an evil body.

The Albigensians at first won respect by their disciplined example, in contrast to the behavior of many self-indulgent and undisciplined "orthodox" clergy of that time. They were at last defeated by the preaching and teaching of St. Bernard and the new order of Dominicans, by a crusade (an early crusade was against these heretics, not against the Moslems) led by Simon de Montfort, and by a rigorous persecution that inaugurated the Inquisition.

Denis de Rougemont in his book, *Love in the Western World,* claims that the repressive measures, ostensibly successful in eliminating the Albigensians, succeeded in driving some of these teachings underground, only to have them rise again as operative elements in the tradition of romantic love in Western civilization. The same ideal of platonic (ideal) love feeding on the romantic agony and exquisite anguish of forbidden or impossible love, and invariably ending in death, is an element of the Albigensian form of Gnosticism and persists still as characteristic of the tradition of romantic love in Western civilization. These same heresies can arise from our *sarx,* our sinful nature, and do not necessarily need the teachings of a defined, established heresy. Nevertheless, the fact remains that any literature of romantic love in the West since the twelfth century, from the tales of Tristram and Isolde, Romeo and Juliet, Lancelot and Guinevere, Petrarch and Laura, and their subsequent parallels, until the "naturalism" reaction in the twentieth century, contains many of the Docetic and Gnostic elements present in the Manichaeism of the twelfth century heresies. C. S. Lewis has also ably shown the religious roots of the romantic love tradition in Western civilization.[5]

The flight from any responsible "incarnational" love is characteristic of the literature of romantic love. Hardly a single example of romance in married love exists in all of the Western romantic love tradition. Lovers scarcely know each other and are more in love with love than with each other. Death always intervenes before there is any significant chance for two people to know each other as they really are. Death, therefore, obscures the need for self-giving kind of love (*agape*) to supplement and save this romantic love (*eros*) from its essential preoccupation with self and its idealized projections. The end or destiny of romantic love as a religion is always death, either of the love or of the lovers. Thus death obscures for its adherents the essential self-centeredness and flight that is characteristic of romantic love. All seem to end in daggers, poison, or mutual suicide. The twentieth century has a rather sentimentalized version of this fatal end: marriage. (*"Oh how we danced on the night we were wed. . . ."* Romantic love can last only until marriage.)

The comic strip figures of Steve Canyon and Judge Parker each lost their central focus when they married. Secondary, unmarried figures, who could provide romantic interest lost by marriage, gradually replaced them as central characters.

It would be difficult to exaggerate the pain, suffering, and broken marriages of countless people who have been misled over the centuries into thinking that "true" love is always some other, impossible, forbidden love. This love feeds the essential romantic agony, exquisite anguish, self-pity, and death (literal or symbolic, as in marriage seen as death) that characterizes "true" love in eight hundred years of romantic tales. In contrast to the escape of Docetism, Christianity promises redemption and internal change that enables two people to love each other in all their concreteness.

We can see by these examples that heresies have been and will be perennial. We can also see that they are often encouraged by something lacking or something corrupt in conventional orthodoxy. Great harm and lasting damage result when orthodoxy responds to heresies, dangerous though they be, with the singularly un-Christian spirit that has been so much a part of the church's contention against these aberrations. The Crusade against the Albigensians marked a departure from the general policy that allowed for excommunication but forbade physical penalties. This principle was enunciated by St. Bernard (1090-1153): *"Fides suadenda, non imponenda"* ("Faith persuaded, not imposed.")

Final acceptance of the canon of scripture helped to save Christians from teachers like Marcion who would subtract from the gospel, and from those like Montanus who would add to it their own idiosyncratic and exotic teachings. The more explicit creeds of the fourth century helped to mark the boundaries and limits of what we can authentically teach about God who is Father, Son and Holy Spirit, without sacrificing something of the redemptive experience of Christians.

Without these limits, Christianity would certainly have been lost as it became divided into infinitely diverse distortions, subtractions, additions and absorptions of human inferences and historical systems. It would have been like a trail into a swamp. But, as necessary and as lastingly valuable as these limits are, they produced yet another heresy: the tendency of orthodoxy to define itself as simple assent to the creeds. Neither creeds nor correct doctrines are the objects of our faith. They did not die for our salvation. Yet, as faithful guidelines to the inevitable implications of scripture and boundaries for what can be called authentic Christianity, they are far more important than is currently appreciated. They are symbols that point to God but, like dogs being trained to fetch, we look at the trainer's finger rather than toward that to which the finger points. Faithfulness to correct doctrine and loyalty to the creeds is not the same thing as trust in the God whom the creeds describe. This is the perennial temptation of orthodoxy itself. It is like tennis players who mark off the court, put up the net, sit down and call that "tennis." The contemporary fashion in the church, to try to play the theological game without lines or net, does not justify the orthodox in marking off the court and raising the net while neglecting to play the game.

We shall see in the next chapter what issues and experiences were at stake as the lines were drawn concerning the doctrine of the Trinity.

3

The Trinity

Father, we praise you: through your Word and
Holy Spirit you created all things. You reveal your
salvation in all the world by sending to us Jesus
Christ, the Word made flesh. Through your Holy
Spirit you give us a share in your life and love. Fill
us with the vision of your glory, that we may always
serve and praise you, Father, Son, and Holy Spirit.
One God, for ever and ever.[1]

The Christian teaching regarding the doctrine of the Trinity
should not be as daunting and intimidating as many have made
it appear. This is not to say that anyone comprehends the deep
mystery of the Trinity any more than one comprehends the
mystery of birth or why the stomach does not digest itself.
People continue to have children and to eat without exhausting
the mystery in either of these subjects. As humans can learn
more about childbirth and eating without dispelling their final
mystery, Christians can learn more about the Trinity without
comprehending its mystery.

What's the Problem?
If a small boy picks up a pipe wrench and asks, "What is

this?," the first step is to show him what it is for, what it does, what its function is. Similarly, to ask what an answer means, one must relate it to the question it answers. To understand a resolution, one must relate it to the problem it resolves. The first step, then, is to appreciate one of the significant questions to which the Trinity is the answer, a problem resolved by the teaching concerning the Trinity. This problem is called "the one and the many." It is not unique to Christianity. Everyone, everywhere and always, has had to struggle with this problem. It can be illustrated by the following questions:

What place does an individual have in a family? in a tribe?

What place does an individual have in a business? in an army?

What place does a black have in America?

What place does a white have in South Africa?

What place does a political dissenter have in a democracy? in a dictatorship?

What place does a faculty member with unpopular views have in a university?

These are merely some of the forms in which the universal problem of "the one and the many" manifests itself. Solutions vary. Some take the form of parental or autocratic tyranny, tyranny of the majority, tyranny of the minority on the one hand; or divorce, departure, running away, quitting, being fired, establishing a ghetto, starting a revolution or civil war, on the other.

In other words, simple solutions to the one and the many sacrifice the diversity and individuality of the many for an imposed and tyrannical unity of the one, or sacrifice the unity (family, nation, business, club, or church) for the sake of the pluralism and diversity of the many.

Christian faith claims that, by worshiping God, both unity and diversity are possible without sacrificing either. Each alternative to this Christian claim invariably has its own solution to which it gives conscious or unconscious adherence. This claim cannot but appear extravagant; it is not only a claim but also a promise.

What it means to worship God is by no means self-explanatory or self-evident. We must first recover what is meant by "worship" and then go on to identify something of what is meant by "God."

Worship is the way humans resolve the question of identity. "What are human beings that you are mindful of them?" *(Ps. 8:4 NRSV)*. What does it mean to be human? A human is the only animal that wears clothes, feels guilt, the only animal that blushes (and "needs to," according to Mark Twain), the only animal that asks what it means to be, the only animal that it is "shameful to call a beast" (Bishop Stephen Bayne's phrase), the only animal that knows it is to die, the only animal that must decide what sort of animal it is.

Humans inevitably decide this identity question by choosing images, consciously or unconsciously: parents, teachers, famous people (whom we appropriately term "idols" as in "matinee idols" or "celebrity idols"). There is such hunger to have role models, heroes, and exemplars that they are constantly being manufactured by the media, and those who seem to last longer are those who die earlier. Anyone who is perceived to exemplify worth or honor immediately attracts fans or adherents who emulate the object of their admiration or praise by attempting to become like her or him. Celebrity idols have the power to change fashions in clothes, hair styles, and behavior because the underlying dynamic in worship is that we tend to become like what we respect, what we honor, what we deem worthy of praise.

A girls' camp in North Carolina once had a rash of campers lined up at the infirmary asking for crutches and bandages for sprained ankles. An attractive and winsomely confident counselor had fallen and sprained her ankle. The younger, admiring preadolescents had unconsciously identified with and desired to emulate one whom they honored and to whom they attributed worth and dignity, even to the point of imagining themselves also afflicted with sprained ankles.

Any leader who can evoke significant respect and attributions of worth will be followed and emulated. Especially if he or she can bring what seems to be cohesive unity to political diversity, his portrait will be carried and her image revered, not just by adolescents, but by all humans who thirst insatiably for some resolution to the problem of "one and the many." Sometimes it is not a person but an ideology that promises to resolve this dilemma, and the fervor of its adherents is notorious for the religious intensity of its faithful. Yet, only when ideologies have human figures do they have significant power to effect even a temporary resolution (of any sort) to the one and the many.

This is why Roman Caesars tended to deify themselves. All attempted to enforce a unity on the empire, and most attempted to do this with religion. Unity at first took the form of excluding Christianity by persecution. But, as Christianity grew to be the strongest faith in spite of persecution, it was granted legal status. Persecution proved unproductive since the blood of the martyrs was the seed of the church and the vigor of Christianity threatened that unity. Christianity was then declared the official religion by the state in order to preserve and enhance that unity. Subsequently, it was seen to be in the emperor's interest to enforce, an orthodoxy to prevent diversity and schism in the church, which in turn would escalate the centrifugal forces that threatened the unity of the Empire.

Whether for sincere or for cynical motives, successive emperors good and bad (and some of the best—Trajan, Hadrian, Antonius Pius, and Marcus Aurelius—were responsible for persecutions of Christianity) passed through these stages of attempting to undergird the empire's unity by unifying its worship. In modern times massive portraits of dictators are carried about and posted as icons of religious proportions. We rarely understand these issues because we have frequently been given a very narrow and clericalized view of worship which fails, not only to acknowledge the pervasive and universal reality of worship, but also to take into account the biblical understanding of worship's crucial importance and the serious danger of idolatry.

Since we tend to become like what we worship, and since we were created in the image of God, the commandment not to worship "any other gods but me" is not an expression of the jealousy of God for God's sake, but for ours. To bow down before and to become like anything or anyone but God himself is ultimately for us to begin to be recreated in some other image. Things, animals, and other people have historically been the objects of worship, but even the highest of these, other people, is unworthy of our worship.

Any other person—parent, aunt, uncle, celebrity—is an unworthy object of worship. It is like measuring with a flawed ruler, but worse. As a copy of a picture is not as good as the original, so emulations and imitations of Marilyn Monroe and Elvis Presley are pitifully ludicrous and never measure up to the original. Roots of secular humanism lie in the Renaissance with its motto: "Man is the measure of all things." This is the fatal flaw of all humanism: since all persons are flawed, we are measuring with a flawed norm.

But do we then escape these problems when we worship God? Unfortunately, not automatically! There are some descriptions and identifications of God that could be even worse than choosing Mao Zedong to worship: some of the gods of ancient Greece, for example, who exemplified some of the worst of human character traits, fertility gods, and ineffable, unknowable, uncaring deities who, in their inaccessibility, were as cruelly empty as the capricious gods who behaved like self-indulgent adolescents. Worship of such deities results in the imposition of these images on human adherents whose true identity, already distorted by sin, is further corrupted by becoming like such false images.

From its authentic roots in Israel, the Christian church inherited an experience of a just and caring God, the God of Abraham, Isaac, and Jacob, the God who had brought them out of the land of Egypt into freedom. It was never a question simply of "God," but the God who had done this and that. God was and always must be identified in the divine actions. The crucial question is not "Is there a God?" but "What kind of God do we have?" The faithful Christian answer is: the God and Father of our Lord Jesus Christ whom we know by the Holy Spirit.

Thus, the Trinity is essentially God's name: God the Father, God the Son, and God the Holy Spirit, one God. If the worship of God is the resolution of the problem of the "one and the many" that destroys neither the one nor the many, then it must provide the basis for unity without destroying individuality, and affirm individuality without destroying unity. The paradox involved in the "one and three" is never enlightened by inanimate examples such as ice, water, and steam; three leaf clovers; or that the sun is round, hot and light.

The most enlightening path is to keep as close to scripture and the actual saving experiences of Christians as possible. To do otherwise is to worship (and become like) something less than human. Scripture is clear that there is one God. The New Testament cannot be read as producing two additional gods to the God of Abraham. Christ is Lord but not another God. He must go away that "the Counselor, which is the Holy Spirit, whom the Father will send in my name, will come. He will teach you all things, and bring to your remembrance all that I have said to you" (*John 14:26*).

As it is clear that the New Testament teaches nothing of three gods, it is equally clear that there are significant distinctions between Father, Jesus Christ, and the Holy Spirit. They are distinct, they are related, and they are one. How can this be so? The crucial response to this question was hammered out in the fourth century in two Ecumenical (or General) Councils. Here, the limits set for orthodox Christianity have been recognized by virtually the whole church ever since.

On a general level, one can easily understand that if there are three (or more) gods, disunity is not only for now but also forever. There are continuing possibilities of a church being torn asunder by rival allegiances, some to the Father, others to the Son, and still others to the Spirit, if their substantial (essential) identity is denied. The unity of Christian believers is presently and ultimately dependent upon the oneness of God and on the continual worship of "one Lord, one Faith, one Baptism, one God and Father of us all."

We have seen the great threat to Christianity from Gnostic affirmations of a whole series of deities emanating in myriad progressions toward an ultimate, unknowable god. We have also seen the unparalleled contribution of Irenaeus who contended against this attempt to appropriate Christianity into another aspect of Gnostic religion. Irenaeus had considerable help from a sector of the church that was adamantly monotheistic and would tolerate no polytheism.

Monarchians

This sector was called Monarchian (monos - one, arche - rule). Monarchians insisted on retaining the radical monotheism of Christianity. God is one. This commendable approach, however, was not balanced by a comparable appreciation of scripture's clear distinctions between the Father, Jesus Christ, and the Holy Spirit. Monarchianism was widely present in the church before the Council of Nicaea (325) in both Alexandria and Antioch, and today it is among the most popular distortions of Christianity. It is thus important that we understand clearly what is at stake in the Monarchians' laudable desire to hold fast to the faith that Christians worship *one* God and their failure to appreciate the distinctive otherness in Father, Son, and Holy Spirit.

The Monarchians' approach to the problem of the relationship of three "persons" to the one unity was to denigrate the "persons" and their experienced distinctions. The Monarchians were themselves divided between Modalistic Monarchians and Dynamic Monarchians. The latter were essentially Adoptionists; we will leave them to our further discussion of Adoptionism under the Third Ecumenical Council.

The Modalistic Monarchians were so called because they resolved the three-in-one paradox by merging the "three" as mere temporary modes into the "one." They taught that the one God could and did express himself at different times and stages in diverse forms or modes. Thus, for the work of creation God was "Father"; for the work of salvation, God appears as "Son"; and for the work of inspiration as "Holy Spirit."

The advantage of this solution is its neatness and consistency. "Father, Son and Holy Spirit, One God" is simply explained by them as the Father temporarily manifesting himself as the Son and at other times as the Holy Spirit. It is like one person being a spouse, mother, and insurance executive. One objection was noticed immediately, when this resolution was put forward by Sabellius, the most prominent of these Monarchians. If it were the Father who was manifest as Jesus, then, according to Sabellius' teaching, it was, in fact, the Father who was crucified. This heresy was often called "Patripassianism" ("Father-suffered-ism"), in addition to its name "Modalistic Monarchianism" (the persons being only "modes" of the one), or the name we shall be using, "Sabellianism," for its chief proponent. Hence, Modalistic Monarchianism, Patripassianism, and Sabellianism are the same thing.

A second objection to this teaching is its exclusion of the scriptural description of the distinct activities of the second and third persons of the Trinity. The logos is "with God" (*John 1:1*) and is incarnate in Jesus of Nazareth, prays to the Father, seeks to do the Father's will, and clearly makes important distinctions between himself and the Father. Also, he must "go away" *(John 16:7)* for the Holy Spirit to come, and no one can confess him but by the Spirit.

A careful perusal of the scriptural references to each of the persons of the Trinity reveals no theologically precise definition, but there is a clear and consistent affirmation that the unity of the Father, the Son, and the Spirit does not deny their distinctiveness. The teaching concerning the Trinity does not proceed from philosophical concerns but from the saving experiences of God's action as recorded in scripture.

If Sabellius' teaching had won the day, Christians could not now testify at the bedside of a dying person that the kind of merciful God we have known in Jesus Christ is forever the same. Christ is no "temporary manifestation" of how God was or "felt" back then. If this were so, you or I may be so unlucky as to reach that judgment seat on a day that God has a headache and is playing a very different role from the one we've seen in Christ. On the contrary, Christ as the eternal image *(Col. 1:15)* of God, is Alpha and Omega *(Rev. 1:8)*, the beginning and the end. He was no temporary manifestation of God that is or can be superseded. If he were, God would not have been fully revealed in Christ. The Christian claim, hope, faith, promise and assurance is that when we have seen Christ we "have seen the Father" and who God is, not temporarily, but everlastingly.

Suppose a graduate student at New York University told his roommate in great excitement that the girl he was dating was beginning to look like the very girl he wants to marry. "She is so compliant, so responsive, so genuinely interested in what's on my mind that she builds up my confidence and I feel ten feet tall when I'm with her! Mary is in her last year of drama school and is already making a name for herself on the stage."

"That's a coincidence," replied his roommate. "Last year I was dating a girl named Mary, also in drama school, but she was nothing like the person you described. This Mary was fascinating but exhausting. She was so full of energy and her own agenda that I felt gobbled up every time we met. I admired her greatly but she was unbelievably assertive and her own self-confidence made me feel like nothing but an accessory."

The radically different Marys turned out to be one and the same. She was deeply involved in a version of the Stanislavsky acting method in which she was taught to live, think, and "be" the person whose role she was playing. She was now playing Sally Bowles in Van Druten's play *I Am a Camera,* whereas last year she was playing the lead in G.B. Shaw's *St. Joan.* Suppose after they are married she takes on the role of Shakespeare's Lady Macbeth? What chance does he have of knowing *her* if all she ever reveals is a *role* she is acting?

This illustration can serve to point out the dangers of reducing the persons of the Trinity merely to roles or modes that God acts or plays at various times. To believe in a god whose action in Christ is not his everlasting divine nature is to be bereft of any final confidence that God is the same as God's self-revelation in Christ. Sabellian believers, becoming like what they worship, will inevitably resort to being poseurs, persons who affect a particular manner or character as changing circumstances seem to require. This pervasive but pitiful compulsion in contemporary society to create for oneself an image or an identity is a symptom of a religious wasteland that has been given no confidence in a God-given identity.

Sabellianism has some merit in its assertion that God is one. But it sacrifices the diversity that is recorded in scripture of God's eternal self-expression in Christ and in the Spirit.

Sabellianism's oneness (or monism), which is becoming increasingly popular in modern times, renders God impersonal. The expressions of God (Father, Son and Holy Spirit) do not reveal God as God is. Monism is actually no closer to Christianity than dualism is, and it results finally in what is called pantheism, the belief that God is all and all is God.[2] Monism and pantheism will be treated in chapter 10, but it is important to note that they are historically and logically related to Sabellianism.

Worshiping a Sabellian deity would be like having a spouse who only played roles—someone who was a Democrat to Democrats, a Republican to Republicans, Laborite to Laborites and Conservative to Conservatives. There would be no distinction between that person and whatever came along. Such a person would cease to be, in any real sense, an individual. Any disagreement with or affection for this spouse would be absorbed and swallowed up not in personhood, but in process. How different is the biblical portrayal of God creating the world, choosing Israel, judging God's people, sending the prophets, coming in Christ to redeem and save, and being here now in the Holy Spirit as our judge and sanctifier. To show the falseness of Sabellianism is not enough. It is also important to see something deeper and more valuable about safeguarding the eternal integrity of the distinct persons. We have seen that a factor in all worship is the dynamic of emulation and that we are influenced consciously or unconsciously to become like what we worship.

"God is love, and those who abide in love abide in God, and God abides in them." *(1 John 4:16 NRSV).* The very nature of love demands both unity and diversity. That both are in God is crucial for us to become truly loving by worshiping God. The essential nature of love is revealed in the Christian teaching of the Trinity. Love cannot be love except it be a verb, an action. It is impossible even to think "love" except as one pictures an action, or an object that symbolizes an action. God cannot be *love* unless God *loves.* Since God's very nature is love *(1 John 4:8),* God's love is an eternal activity. In its unity the Sabellian deity does not possess the everlasting distinctions that establish this action. Giving and receiving love is essential to the story we have of the Christian God.

The gospel story tells of this giving nature of God's love in the sending of Christ by the Father *(John 3:16).* It tells of the risks of love in the temptations, agony, crucifixion, and death of Christ. It tells of the unconquerable nature and power of that love in the resurrection. It tells of the perfect exchange of perfect love in which the Father gives all in Christ and Christ returns all that is given to the Father (*John 6:37, 39*). It tells of our knowing this love by the Holy Spirit.

To worship the Sabellian deity is to become less rather than more personal. The word most frequently used in the New Testament for worship is *proskuneo,* which means "to bow the knee before." What we bow down to is what we become like. One might say that "to bow the knee" is the posture of contagion whereby we catch something of what we worship. It is thus a matter of our very identity. To worship a Sabellian deity is to be led in an unknown direction. For the Sabellian, what is seen in Christ and what is known of the Father by the Spirit is not truly God, but only roles that God once played. We would miss knowing the self-giving love that God showed in Christ, the unimposed return of that love by Christ, and the spontaneous love that reveals itself in the Holy Spirit. We would become more and more like those people who try to resolve, in tyranny, the one and the many by the kind of "love" that destroys diversity for the sake of unity.

Refuge in roles is a neurotic sanctuary for many people. The apparent safety of exposing oneself only in the functions of parent, lawyer, teacher, boss, or breadwinner can insulate us from knowing and being known, from loving and being loved. When a son or daughter discovers, and is discovered by, a parent in a new relationship, in which the roles of child and parent are no longer necessary and two adult people begin to know each other behind those roles, it is a joy difficult to exaggerate. It is a rare analogy of divine love.

Similarly, if God is known only in modes or roles as the Sabellian teaches, then we cannot know God, or be known by God, on the deepest levels. And not to know is not to love. In contrast, David Jenkins, the Bishop of Durham, sums up for us the implication of the church's trinitarian teaching:

> The Holy Trinity, therefore, symbolizes, focuses, and points to that glorious and saving mystery of God which is the sole source

of our faith, the whole promise of our hope, and the full entice-
ment of our love. God as Holy Trinity is God the universal
Father and source of all being and all blessing who is greater
than great—transcendent over all. Yet this same God as Son and
Savior is one with us in the particularity of our flesh and blood
to overcome that which separates us from God's glory and love.
The God who is greater than great is, in a down-to-earth way,
more loving than love. And it is this same transcendent and
down-to-earth God who is available at all times and in all places
as the Holy Spirit who is both freely transcendent and yet closer
than close—available at the very heart of each one of us and as
the bond of sharing and empowering between us.[3]

4

Arianism: The Three Deities

> To begin with, the Trinity is primarily a fact and not
> a doctrine. And it is a fact which alone brings God
> down to our apprehension and into our experience.
> That God reveals himself to us in his personal divine
> Word and imparts himself to us by his personal divine
> Spirit is the basis of all Christian knowledge of God.
> **William Porcher DuBose**

We have seen the division of all heresies into two main groups:
Adoptionist and Docetic. We have also approached this division
from the human factor, self-centeredness on the one hand and the
desire to escape the conditions of being human on the other.

A further extension of these pairings that can be helpful is
the contrast between the two patriarchal cities, Alexandria and
Antioch. In philosophy, Antioch was more congenial with the
Aristotelian approach, while Alexandria tended to be Platonic.

It has often been said (somewhat too simply) that each of us
is basically an Aristotelian or a Platonist. An Aristotelian looks
at a chair and sees its substance or essence as wood, metal,
or plastic, something knowable by the five senses: smelling,
touching, seeing, hearing, or tasting. A Platonist, on the other
hand, sees the substance or essence of a chair as idea, the idea

in the mind of its maker that shaped it to be a chair and not a desk or table. For the Platonist, the wood, metal, or plastic—what most modern people are likely to call its "substance"—are mere temporary manifestations of the eternal *form* of chair, which is its true substance.

With its Greek atmosphere, Alexandria thought in terms of ontological (concerning being) union, whereas Antioch with its more Judaic background stressed the power of moral example. Religiously, Alexandria was mystical as Antioch was rational. Alexandria emphasized metaphysics while Antioch was more interested in ethics. Scholars in Alexandria used an allegorical interpretation of scripture, while the Antiochene approach to scripture focused on the literal text.

We shall see how these two cities and their successive leaders approached the questions of the Trinity and of Christ's person from quite contrasting concerns. These concerns have important affinities with Docetism and Adoptionism. Alexandrians leaned, as a rule, toward a willingness to sacrifice the full humanity of Christ, and Antioch tended to produce an Adoptionist Christ, sacrificing the unity between God and humanity in Christ.

It could be helpful (provided we understand these pairings in a general way) to look at a list of how the fourth-century world was divided in its approach to the teaching of the Trinity and of Christ.

Docetic	Adoptionist
Alexandria	Antioch
Platonic	Aristotelian
Greek	Judaic
Unity	Diversity
Allegorical use of scripture	Literal use of scripture
Philosophical (metaphysical)	Ethical
Mystical	Rational
Gnostic	Legalistic
No real incarnation	No real atonement
Spiritual	Historical

Sometimes heresies can be so complex that they involve aspects of both types. Such a heresy is Arianism.

Arius

In church history Arius (ca. 256-336) has been called the "Heresiarch" or "chief heretic." As we shall see, he certainly taught aspects of both basic types. The first step is to see how he differed from Sabellius. While the Sabellians resolved the "one and the many" by denying the many for the sake of unity, so Arius sacrificed ultimate unity by postulating one superior God with two subordinate deities. In his teaching he combined some of the worst of Antioch and Alexandria. Although he was influenced deeply by a succession of Adoptionist theologians in Antioch, he also made use of certain teachings of one of the most influential thinkers in the early church, Origen.

Origen (ca. 185-254) was born and reared in the intellectual center of the ancient world, Alexandria. Two incidents in Origen's life make him especially memorable. He was an intensely committed young man who was quite willing to die for his faith (perhaps too willing, his mother believed). A persecution of Christians in 203 claimed the life of Origen's heroic father, Leonides. During a later persecution Origen was saved from the general execution of confessing Christians because his mother hid his clothes. He was willing to be martyred, but not while naked.

The other incident was his attempt to resolve his struggle for chastity by literally making himself "a eunuch for Christ's sake" *(Matt. 19:12)*. This action was to mar not only his body but also his reputation and subsequent influence. Irregularly ordained, he was not recognized by the bishop in Alexandria and spent his later life in Caesarea, dying as a result of treatment in jail during persecution.

His unusual life should not obscure from us his prodigious contribution to the development of Christian doctrine. The city of Alexandria was the intellectual capital of the world, and it remained so until it was engulfed by the Moslems in 642 and its incomparable library destroyed. Origen was one of the greatest minds and most prolific writers that the early church produced and few have surpassed him since. His writings became a mine for the orthodox, who were greatly aided by the work he had done on the relationship of the persons in the Godhead, and for heretics who amplified the Gnostic and Docetic tendencies that could also be found in Origen.

This latter emphasis was exemplified in the approach of Arius who gave his name to the most pervasive heresy of the fourth century, Arianism. Under the Alexandrian influence, Arius assumed that God could in no way be as intimately related to people and to the world as is described in the Hebrew scriptures. For the Alexandrian deity, there can be none of the intimacy that we see in the call of Abraham, no immanence such as we find in the dialogues with Moses, no immediate and unmediated involvement with God's people as is reflected in the prophets and Psalms.

Instead, Arius was eager to preserve the unity of the Godhead against the surrounding polytheism. He thought that the unity of God could be preserved only by excluding all distinctions from within the divine nature, making Jesus Christ and the Holy Spirit into two inferior deities. He seized upon each scriptural formulation that suggested inferiority or a subordinate status for Christ. "Why do you ask me about what is good? One there is who is good" (Matt. 19:17); ". . . for the Father is greater than I" (John 14:28). ". . . nevertheless not my will but thine be done" (Luke 22:42). In addition to arguments from many texts, a different and lesser deity than God himself fitted the Alexandrian assumption (and Docetic tendency) that it was both inappropriate and impossible for God himself to take the bodily form of a man, to be born of a woman, to be hungry and thirsty, to weep, to suffer, and to die.

Jesus Christ was, according to Arius, just such an intermediate deity between God and humanity, one who was neither fully God nor fully human. The very fact that scripture repeatedly refers to the relationship as "Father and Son" implied, for Arius, both the inferiority of the latter and a priority of the Father *before* the Son was "begotten." Arius took the symbolism of Father literally, inferring the kind of relationship human fathers have with human sons, and saw Christ as a subordinate deity other than the Father.

Since Christ is the logos (Word) incarnate, and the logos was God's agent in creation, he could rightly be called God. Since he was the Son, he was less than the Father. And since there was a "time when he was not," Arius thought he was in some sense a creature and certainly not eternal.

Arius was described by contemporaries as tall and grave with a commanding presence. He was one of the best known presbyters in the city and had a reputation for asceticism. He was in charge of a church in an economically important suburb of Alexandria (where the huge granaries from which corn was shipped to Rome were situated), when charges of heresy were made against him to his bishop, Alexander. The bishop claimed against Arius that the Son is equal to the Father and explained the relationship between the two by using the word *homoousios,* meaning "of the same substance."

This word was to become the battleground fought over from this event in 318 until 381. It involved the entire Empire as well as the church. Some fifteen emperors, five popes, scores of patriarchs, hundreds of bishops, and fervent street mobs took sides. It was front-page news of the day. The issue itself was never isolated as a purely theological or religious matter, but one intricately involved in animosities, personalities, rivalries, matters of state, and economics.

The argument called forth the First General Council in 325 at Nicaea to settle the question posed between Arius and his bishop, Alexander, centering on this word *homoousios.* The council was a victory for Alexander and defeat for the Arians. It did not, however, settle the issue. Over the next fifty-six years, twelve more councils were held that largely supported the views of Arius, but since their decrees did not prove to be acceptable to the general church, the gatherings were not counted as among the General (Ecumenical) Councils. The matter was not resolved until the Second General Council of Constantinople in 381.

Instead of Athanasius' term *homoousios* (of the same substance), Arius used the term *homoiousios* meaning of *like* substance, that the Son was not of the same substance, very God of very God, with the Father, but was of *like* substance. The whole argument has been ridiculed by some as upsetting the entire church and empire over an *iota,* the smallest letter in the Greek alphabet, giving rise to the saying "It doesn't make an iota's difference."

It is, however, a crucial matter. Professor Paul Lehmann of Union Seminary exclaimed in his lectures, "The future of the Christian church hung by an *iota!*" The very nature and essence of the Christian faith was at stake on this issue. Could the struggle have been avoided? When one considers the manifold texts that refer to Jesus Christ and to the Father and to the Holy Spirit, the question was bound to arise, as it will continue to do. When Jesus asks, "What do you think of the Christ? Whose son is he?" *(Matt. 22:42),* it is a question not only to the disciples but to each subsequent generation.

We have seen how the answers were given from two extreme positions, one Docetic and the other Adoptionist, either of which, if followed, would have destroyed the possibility of the experience Christians have of Christ. The Docetic twist would serve to encourage any flight from humanity and history into a "religious" escape, a mystical ecstasy, and death.

An Adoptionist Christ, on the other hand, gives us a picture of the man, Jesus, who succeeded in obeying the law as we should, and whose gospel is to try harder. This doctrine appeals to our thirst for self-justification, nurtures and encourages our tendencies to make a gospel of freedom into a religion of control, and helps to insulate (and isolate) our self-centered selves with the armor of our own righteousness, thereby maintaining and sustaining our self as center.

Each of these answers to "What do you think of Christ?" stems from conditions of our human nature: a tendency to flee life for death, on the one hand, and a tenacious desire "to be as gods" on the other. Each heretical answer not only results from twisted historical teachings but feeds on the least worthy desires of the human heart.

The Arian denial of *homoousios* (one substance), while not as recognizably gross a heresy as Docetism or Adoptionism, nevertheless has within it the inevitable logic of both. In denying *homoousios* Arius denies the oneness of God and Christ. Even if one is "in Christ," one is not yet reconciled with or at one with God. This latter mistake represents the influence on Arius of his Antioch teachers who lacked a doctrine of atonement (the at-one-ment reconciliation of sinners with God effected by Christ). Orthodox Christians insisted that to be in Christ is to be at one with God. Thus, to be baptized is to be "a member of Christ, the child of God, and an inheritor of the kingdom of heaven."[2]

Origen influenced Arius in the matter of subordinationism, the inference from texts of scripture that Jesus Christ and (by implication) the Holy Spirit were lesser or subordinate deities. It is the opposite solution to the "one and the many" formula that we have seen in Sabellianism. In the latter, the "many" or the distinctions are lost in the unity of the Godhead. With Arius the "one and the many" dilemma is resolved by losing the "one" unity and postulating three deities, albeit unequal.

The strength of Arius' teaching is that it seems faithful to the many texts which quite obviously disclose distinctions between the Father and the Son, and depict the deference Jesus pays to the Father. "How," the Arians asked, "could Jesus pray to the Father if he were not different from the Father?"

It is essential for anyone possessing any sense of obligation to orthodoxy to acknowledge the heavy weight of Arius's argument. The fact is that, on first glance, it would seem that he has many more scriptural texts on his side than on the side of *homoousios,* a term that is not to be found in scripture. (This fact was repeatedly made by the Arians to telling effect. *Homoousios* was *agrapha*—"unwritten.")

The best way to answer these weighty arguments is to examine the teaching of one of the greatest and most heroic figures in the whole history of the Christian church.

Athanasius

Athanasius (295-373) was a protege of Bishop Alexander and, as a young deacon, went with the bishop to the great Council at Nicaea. Athanasius had already written a short pamphlet, *De Incarnatione,* when he was in his early twenties. Although in later life he produced more elaborate writings against the Arians, this brief work of his youth is a remarkable document that has continued to edify and inspire readers throughout subsequent centuries.

Although written before the Arian controversy began, *De Incarnatione* was and remains the classically powerful yet simple anti-Arian statement. C. S. Lewis made the following comment on this timeless work of the young Athanasius:

> When I first opened his *De Incarnatione* I soon discovered by a very simple test that I was reading a masterpiece. I knew very little Christian Greek except that of the New Testament and I had expected difficulties. To my astonishment I found it almost as easy as Xenophon; and only a mastermind could, in the fourth century, have written so deeply on such a subject with such classical simplicity. Every page I read confirmed this impression. His approach to the Miracles is badly needed today, for it is the final answer to those who object to them as 'arbitrary and meaningless violations of the laws of Nature.' They are here shown to be rather the re-telling in capital letters of the same message which Nature writes in her crabbed cursive hand; the very

operations one would expect of Him who was so full of life that when He wished to die He had to 'borrow death from others.' The whole book, indeed, is a picture of the Tree of Life—a sappy and golden book, full of buoyancy and confidence. We cannot, I admit, appropriate all its confidence today. We cannot point to the high virtue of Christian living and the gay, almost mocking courage of Christian martyrdom, as a proof of our doctrines with quite that assurance which Athanasius takes as a matter of course. But whoever may be to blame for that it is not Athanasius.[3]

Athanasius himself was more of a pastor than a theologian. He did not begin with philosophical or theological concerns but with a passion for human souls. His approach, like that of Irenaeus, has accurately been termed "soteriological." That is to say, he was primarily concerned with how humans are saved. Athanasius' tenacity in asking the biblical question, "How can one be saved?" kept all theological speculation tied to the essential act of God in Christ. It is difficult to improve on his own words.

It was in the power of none other to turn the corruptible to incorruption except the Savior Himself, who had at the beginning made all things out of nothing; none other could create anew the likeness of God's image for men except the Image of the Father; none other could render the mortal immortal except the Lord Jesus Christ who is Life itself; none could teach men the Father and destroy the worship of idols except the Word who orders all things and is alone the true only-begotten Son of the Father.[4]

In addition, Athanasius emphasized a theme that was to become more characteristic of Christianity in the East than in the West. A quote that exemplifies something of the essence of his teaching is: "God became man in order that we might become God."[5] This basic thirst "to be as gods" by pride and disobedience is transformed in grace and love by God's restoring us in Christ to the image in which we were made. "Beloved, we are God's children now; it does not yet appear what we shall be, but we know that when he appears, we shall be like him; for we shall see him as he is" (*1 John 3:2*).

From this perspective of salvation the "gospel" of Arius is simply irrelevant. I have seen this essential bankruptcy of Arianism acted out in classroom debates. I have divided classes into groups of nine in which two are to defend Athanasius against the seven representing Arius' position. The same result was enacted with each successive group. The Arians invariably had the better of the argument until or unless the Athanasians asked the soteriological question, "How can salvation be accomplished?" Then, and then alone, the teaching of Athanasius was seen to describe most fully the event that fulfilled the experience described in the Old Testament, was recorded in the New Testament, and even now is accessible to those who worship Father, Son, and Holy Spirit, one God.

The test of worship must always be applied to doctrine. What happens when, in Arian fashion, we worship Father, Son, and Holy Spirit, one ultimately unknown and unknowable, and the other two, lesser deities? The "dynamic of emulation" that is the imitating principle of worship would render us ultimately divided, while any love that is discerned in Christ and the Holy Spirit is external to God.

What do we become like when we worship the Arian deities? The quality of dependent servant love shown in Christ is relegated to a lesser status, thus feeding and nurturing our pride and self-centeredness and its resistance to ever becoming dependent on anyone but ourselves. Athanasius taught that the giving and bestowing of love that we see in the unity of God himself is not a lesser love. Philip Turner writes:

> Simply stated he held that it is of the eternal nature of God to bestow, present, or give himself. The Son is fully God because God the Father eternally bestows or gives to him all that he is, yet dependent because all that he has comes from the Father.

Similarly the Father is dependent upon the Son; he refuses to force the return of what is given . . . This dependence, however, is not one of imperfection—it is "begotten" by love, and in love the dependent Son gives back all that he is given to the Father. All that is given is returned. God thus lives and is love. His inner life eternally is one of giving, receiving, and returning, and all this takes place in and through the Spirit. Between Father, Son, and Spirit there is a coinherence, a total presence, a giving, receiving, and returning and all this takes place in and through the Spirit.[6]

This concept of a "dependent" factor in divine love needs some amplification. Not only does it appear to contradict much we have been taught in psychology about the immaturity of dependent love, but it also runs counter to our tenacious resistance to the risk and humility of dependence. The wisest of counsellors have pointed out three general steps in maturity: 1) the dependence of infancy; 2) the independence of adolescence; and 3) the creative dependence of mature love, when one is able to take the risk of allowing a dependence to develop without control of or by another.

There seems to be some dynamic in us all that resists ever needing, or being in any way dependent on, another. It is the cause of much of our loneliness,and our shallow and inadequate friendships. The neurotic urge to control other people—spouses, children, employees, friends—has led therapists to make a technical term of the word "control."

The opposite "letting go" relationship of the Father and the Son as shown in scripture has been interpreted by Arians as if the dependency of the Son upon the Father ("Father, if thou art willing, remove this cup from me; nevertheless not my will, but thine, be done." *Luke 22:42*) marked an inferior, because subordinate, position of the Son. This was seen to justify the Arian denial that Christ was of the same substance (*homoousios*) with the Father.

Is it not appropriate to suggest that those who throughout

church history read graceful dependence as weakness will also read the biblical story as Arians do? When one is still in the persistent adolescent stage of clinging to one's own independence, is it not an offensive vulnerability for Christ to "empty himself and take the form of a servant" (*Phil. 2:7*)? To use the biblical examples of Christ's apparent weakness ("Jesus wept" *John 11:35*), his dependence upon the Father ("The Father is greater than I" *John 14:28*) and his relinquishing of control ("nevertheless, not as I will but as thou wilt" *Matt. 26:39*) as support for Arius' claims, is evidence not merely of the mistakes of the mind but also of failure of the heart. To claim that Christ must be a lesser deity to the Father because of the dependent quality of his love is to remove this action of love and its creatively dependent nature from God himself.

The insight that being called to a subordinate position is not a denial of equality with one's superiors is one of the reassuring treasures of the Christian faith. Where Christianity has informed the culture, officials (no matter how exalted) have a sense of being public *servants*. Jesus told his disciples: "But I am among you as one who serves" (*Luke 22:27*). Subordinate positions are transformed by Christianity, providing a dignity and equality that reflects the equality of the Father and the Son.

The pope has as one of his titles "Servant of the Servants of God," and every year he washes the feet of those of "inferior" ranks to show the equality that God's love in Christ has brought to all levels. (This tradition of personal dignity essential for authentic public life is not impervious to human sin. It is said that the grace in the phrase "the servant of the servants" depends upon whether in Latin the dative [servant *to* the servants] or the genitive [of all the servants, I am *the* servant] case is used.)

Some mistakenly assume that the adolescent clinging to independence and the fear of mature dependence is a quantitative matter of birthdays, and that time or education will correct it. This mistake is not as much an intellectual one as it is an emotional one, not an error of the mind but an error of the heart. What was saved by Athanasius was thus essential to Christianity, not just theologically but religiously and pastorally. If Arianism had been accepted by the church we would have been cruelly deprived of that picture of self-giving, dependent love we see in the life of Jesus as part of that ultimate love our families, friends, and enemies so desperately need from us and we from them.

The cruelty implicit in the Arian heresy can also be seen by a comment in the newspaper, *Episcopal Life,* by a writer who hated the story of the crucifixion because it seemed to be nothing more than a terrible example of "child abuse" for the Father to send his Son to be an innocent victim for the sins of others. If the Arians had prevailed (as they obviously have in this person's mind) then how could such a charge be denied? Without the orthodox teaching of the same substance (*homoousios*) of Father and Son, the very nature of the love disclosed on the cross is denied. Our own suffering is thus cut off from its redemptive hope in the suffering of Christ.

The First General Council of Nicaea in 325 providentially condemned the teaching of Arius and inserted into its creed the affirmation: "very God of very God, begotten, not made, being of one substance with the Father." This Nicene Creed was not fully accepted until the Council of Constantinople in 381, but it established, at least in principle and in form, if not yet fully in the hearts of those who recite it, the orthodox Christian faith.

It is a mistake, however, to assume that these Ecumenical Councils, taken for granted in subsequent history by Roman Catholics, Eastern Orthodox, Anglican, Methodist, Lutheran and Reformation churches, were established by any simple, peaceful process. They were authoritative General (Ecumenical) Councils only in retrospect. The victory of Athanasius over the Arians at Nicaea, with the explicit backing and support of the Emperor was not to last long. As noted above, twelve intervening councils still struggled with this yet unestablished resolution to the "one and the many."

Athanasius himself was banished five times after Nicaea for holding to his views "against all the world" (his epitaph: *Athanasius contra mundum*), as successive emperors responded to or used the changing tides of Arian and orthodox influence in attempts to establish uniformity in the empire. The battle against Arianism in its many forms was not settled, but only begun, at Nicaea.

What eventually established the victory of Athanasius and Nicaea was the support of three Eastern theologians, the great Cappadocians, whom we shall treat in the next chapter.

5

The Cappadocians

Basil had admired the hermits, but he had shrewdly asked, "If you continue to live alone, whose feet will you wash?"[1]

Three brilliant men who lived in the fourth century in Cappodocia in Asia Minor were instrumental in overcoming the Arian influence that had undermined the initial victory of Athanasius over Arius at Nicaea. They were Basil of Caesarea (330-379), Gregory of Nazianzus (329-389), and Gregory of Nyssa (died ca. 394).

The sermons that Gregory of Nazianzus preached in Constantinople from 379 to 381 have been credited with helping turn the tide in favor of Nicaea against Arianism at the Council of Constantinople. The son of a bishop, Gregory was a contemporary of Basil's at the University of Athens.

Both eloquent and learned, Basil of Caesarea, the older brother of Gregory of Nyssa, also had a wide reputation for personal holiness. He was at once sensitive and willing to contend in theological controversies in which he was especially effective against the leading Arians of the day. He established a huge complex of hospitals and hostels for the poor and impressed upon Eastern monasticism a structure and ethos which prevails today.

The younger brother, Gregory of Nyssa, although deposed and exiled from his episcopal see by the Arians, was restored to his position in 378 on the death of the Arian emperor, Valens, in time to be a dominant figure in the Council of Constantinople.

Any mention of these Cappodocians should not omit Macrina, the remarkable sister of Basil and Gregory of Nyssa. She was the founder of a great monastery, helped raise another younger brother, Peter, who also became a bishop, and, according to Gregory's biography of her, taught the brothers theology and the divine purposes behind sorrows and disasters. Together, these Cappodocian leaders made the triumph of Nicaea over Arianism possible.

One of the significant reasons for the fifty-nine year difficulty in defeating Arianism was that the views of Athanasius sounded in Eastern ears like Sabellianism. This modalistic reduction of Son and Holy Spirit to mere manifestations or roles of the Father is actually enhanced by insisting on the sameness of Father and Son. The term *homoousios,* which established the essential identity of Father and Son, had been declared heretical in a "catholic" (later to be recognized as orthodox) Synod of Antioch in 269. How is it that *homoousia* is heretical in 269 and orthodox in 325? Can ancient uncouth become so soon good?

The answer is that *homoousios* (the sameness of Father and Son in essence) is the way Sabellians would justify their claim that the Father was incarnate and suffered in the *role* of Christ, therefore this sameness (*homoousios*) had to be denied in 269 when the church was distinguishing the gospel from Sabellianism. However, in 325, when the Arians claimed that Jesus Christ was a different deity from the Father, and thereby denied their substantial identity, this sameness had to be asserted against the Arians' three deities. All of the trinitarian heresies can be divided between Sabellianism and Arianism, between modalistic unity and tritheistic pluralism, between the "solutions" of the one or of the many.

For a long time the Cappadocians suspected the *homoousios* party of Sabellianism, which, with some justification, was considered by the Eastern church to be the characteristic heresy of the West. A way had to be found to explain the concept *homoousios* without falling into Sabellianism (modalism).

Thus the word *hypostasis* was introduced to signify the distinct and diverse realities of Father, Son, and Holy Spirit, while *homoousos* was retained to signify their unity. *Hypostasis* allowed for the eternal significance of the three persons of the Trinity not as mere manifestations or roles but as permanent personal expressions of God. The formula is "one *ousia* in three *hypostaseis*, Father, Son, and Holy Spirit." The word *ousia* (substance, in general) was used for the whole essential reality which is God, while the word *hypostasis* (substance, in particular) was used for each of the three persons by which God is disclosed and known.

On the surface this seemed a simple solution, but considerable confusion resulted as to what the terms meant as they were translated from Greek to Latin. The difficulty lay in the fact that *ousia* comes from the word "to be" in Greek and is translated as "substance" or "essence." *Hypostasis* is derived from a term meaning "to exist" or "to subsist" and is translated as "person." *Ousia* and *hypostasis* were so close in meaning that they had often been used interchangeably. But there was an important distinction. For instance, a man and a woman are particular existencies or persons (*hypostaseis*) who share a common humanity (*ousia*). Thus, *ousia,* implied a general, undifferentiated, underlying reality, whereas *hypostasis* came to mean a particular reality (man or woman), not the underlying essence (humanity).

The relationship of marriage is a good way to illustrate the importance of this distinction. To deny the distinctions of gender between women and men (their *hypostaseis*) would be Sabellian. To deny their common humanity would be Arian. One error destroys the exquisite love and joy that springs from the distinction between men and women (Sabellian); the other denigrates and subordinates one of them as essentially different from and lesser than the other (Arian).

History is replete with examples of tragic attempts to resolve "the one and the many" by people who have never heard of Sabellius or Arius. Positions of some modern radical feminists are not at all immune to these cruel alternatives. At times women's equality of being (*ousia*) has been violated in Arian fashion by women being relegated to an inferior humanity. On the other hand, the reaction that denies the distinctiveness (*hypotasis*) of women and men, in order to preserve their equality and essential (*ousia*) unity, is the Sabellian solution. This latter "solution" is sometimes pressed so far as to forfeit the differences that in no way need imply lack of equality.

Not only genders but also children fall victim to this tension. Sears' catalogue carries commodities labelled "Good," "Better," and "Best," but it would be deeply flawed Arian parents who would rank their children "Good," "Better," or "Best," despite significant differences among them. Yet it is important to note that human frailty has often produced such rankings from the time of Jacob, who "loved Joseph more than any other of his children . . . but when his brothers saw that their father loved him more than all his brothers, they hated him" *(Gen. 37:3-4)*. This is why we were prepared for a messiah who, in his relationship to the Father, showed us a love that denies neither differences nor equality among the recipients of authentic love.

In this way we can begin to understand the importance of these terms: *ousia* for the unity of the God we worship (and become like) and *hypostasis* for the permanent and everlasting personal expressions of Father, Son, and Holy Spirit. The Council of Constantinople established these terms as crucial to safeguard the Christian experience of the triune God, to be faithful to scripture, to know the meaning of true love, and to avoid cruel alternatives.

A problem arose, however, in the translation of these terms

from Greek into Latin. There was only one word in Latin, *substantia*, to translate both *ousia* and *hypostasis*. This caused a great deal of confusion and misunderstanding. When the Greeks spoke of three *hypostaseis* the Latins thought they meant three substances and accused them of Arianism. On the other hand, the Latin denial of three *hypostaseis* seemed to the Greeks to be a stubborn reaffirmation of Sabellianism. The situation was not unlike a husband and wife who have mistakenly switched controls on their electric blanket. She turns hers up to get warm and he turns his down to get cool. They continue these switched signals until one is burning up while the other is freezing.

Athanasius and the Cappadocians used great magnanimity and patience to untangle the wires. As Athanasius reassured the Cappadocians that he was not Sabellian, and the Cappadocians convinced the Western church that they were not Arian or tritheists, it was agreed to use these two terms in Greek for the unity (*ousia*) and distinctions (*hypostaseis*), while in Latin another word *persona* would be used to translate *hypostasis*. Hence, the Latin *una substantia, tres personae* (one substance, three persons).

It is surprising that the Greeks did not use their word *prosopon* instead of *hypostasis*. *Prosopon* is a rough equivalent to the Latin *persona* from which we get the English word "person." The familiar masks worn by actors in Greek drama were called *prosopon*, and if used to describe the persons of the Trinity, it would almost perfectly describe the Sabellian reduction of Christ and the Holy Spirit to mere roles played by the Father.

This agreement to use these terms was a rare example of the magisterial minds and spirits of Athanasius and the Cappadocians. It was hammered out at a council in Alexandria in 362 (during one of the times Athanasius was not banished) and thus paved the way for what became the Second General Council at Constantinople in 381.

The word *persona* (translated into English as "person") can itself cause trouble. It is a mistake to think that the word "person" with all its modern connotations had the meaning it now possesses when it was first used to illustrate this mystery. On the contrary, the church found itself in the same predicament then as it does today when attempting to translate scripture into languages that have had no experience of the Christian faith. They have no words to correspond to the experiences that arise from Christianity. There is no word in Swahili for "atonement," and no word in Japanese for "guilt," the nearest to it being something akin to "shame" (which is quite different from "guilt").

Scholars have pointed out that because the Latin word *persona* was used to denote the Persons of the Trinity, the word began to take on much of what is meant today in the romance languages by "personal" and to carry a connotation that was not fully present before it was used in the Christian creeds. The importance of this trinitarian view of "person" in the crucial issues of contemporary times is shown by Gerald Bray.

> Today we need to reassert that *personhood* does not mean *individuality* but a capacity for relationship. Dogs and cats are individuals, but they are not persons, and no person can find his or her fulfilment in isolation or selfishness. The members of the Trinity show us what being a person means—the Father gives himself by offering his Son in love for the world, the Son gives himself by being sacrificed in love to the Father for the world, and the Holy Spirit gives himself by presenting the Father and the Son to us in love. Self-sacrifice is the only way to perfect self-fulfilment and happiness in the peace of God.

> The Trinity teaches us, moreover, that our existence as persons is dependent on the inner being of God. It is because we are created in his image and likeness that we have a capacity for relationship, which means that our primary relationship must always be with him. In the Trinity we see the sacred tie of kinship (Father and Son) perfectly balanced by the equally sacred Spirit. The ancients knew that a love relationship between two

was imperfect; it required a third to give it balance and fulfilment. Love between two would be self-devouring and destructive, but the third Person, dwelling in complete equality with the other two, provides the balance needed for a complete expression of the essence of God.[3]

Reinhold Niebuhr was fond of warning that "In the beginning God created man in his own image and ever since man has sought to return the compliment." We tend to do this with the word *prosopon* or "person." We learn in an age of faith what it is to be human by worshiping God in whose image lies our true identity and personhood, but in a secular age we tend to project onto God what the culture assumes to be "personal." Like democracy's being described as "the worst form of government save all the alternatives," so the use of personal attributes to describe the Trinity is the worst medium save all the alternatives. Personal attributes imputed to the *personae* of the Trinity must be sharply understood to be far more, not less, than *a person* in any human sense that we have known.[4]

The word "substance" as the translation of *ousia* and *substantia* brings difficulties of a different sort into the twentieth century. Its meaning in the fourth century had nothing of the material connotation it does for us as "basic material," or "any type of matter of a specific chemical compound, such as oak, concrete, plastic." The rarer meaning such as the "substance of an argument" is closer to what is meant in the creed. Our word "essence" is even closer.

To settle this crucial matter by setting limits against both Docetism and Adoptionism, which in their trinitarian forms express themselves as Sabellianism and Arianism, was a great accomplishment for the church. These distortions are both historical, in the sense of the general slant given by the opposing schools of Alexandria and Antioch, and personal, in the sense that each panders to the desire of the human will to escape or to establish its self-centeredness. Considering the bizarre cultic distortions besetting the early Christian church in its fight to preserve the integrity of the gospel message, the contribution of these two councils is difficult to exaggerate.

Christians now had what Irenaeus and Athanasius had lacked: creedal backing against those distortions of the faith that are ultimately and devastatingly cruel to their adherents. A result of the Councils of Nicaea and Constantinople was the Nicene Creed. (Some scholars have urged that we call it by the name of both councils for the sake of accuracy.) In the twentieth century it is easy to be ungrateful for or unmindful of the hard-won victories represented in this creed and the often unacknowledged protection it has afforded us through the ages.

Having acknowledged that accomplishment, we must, at the same time, realize what these councils did not do. The mystery of the Trinity was not dispelled. We do not explain but only assert in this creed that we believe "in one God, the Father Almighty . . . And in one Lord Jesus Christ. . .[and] in the Holy Ghost . . . who with the Father and the Son together is worshipped and glorified." The councils did not put limits on God but established safety barriers for our understanding of mystery and gift.

All our language here must be understood as symbolic, as standing for and pointing to something more. There are those in every age who share in the literalistic Antiochian approach and are too seldom able to discern the meaning of a symbol. To discuss the Trinity with such people is like the frustration a dog owner experiences as he points to the pet's ball and the dog looks at the owner's finger. The opposite error, corresponding to the "religious" interests of the Alexandrian approach, is to look for the ball without any direction or any pointers, as if simply by being religious we can find God while ignoring all maps and teachings leading to God.

A great victory was achieved in these two councils over some unfortunate Arian symbols without reverting to the equally unfortunate Sabellian symbols. For the first time the church had a valuable, explicit set of limits that could be called orthodoxy.

However, a new problem accompanied that very victory: the temptation of orthodoxy to become a new heresy.

Orthodoxy as Idolatry

When orthodox limits had been authoritatively determined by the church and had received the backing of state and emperor, with power to coerce and punish false teaching, a great temptation occurred. Facing exile or banishment, many began to assent to the words or to the formula without in the least affirming what these symbols implied. In reading carefully the history of these centuries one is struck by what a rare thing orthodoxy was. The heresies served a negative purpose by compelling the church to make explicit what was truly of the Christian faith. Such negative contributions we have noticed in Marcion and the early Adoptionists. But even among the greatest positive contributors to the eventually ordered orthodox formulations were such figures as Origen and Tertullian who were themselves, on some issues, seriously misleading. History does not disclose a large, well-established body of orthodox Christians surrounded by a few creative, courageous, and venturesome free thinkers whom the unimaginative and conventional orthodox condemned (as is the popular modern point of view). On the contrary, one can point to only a handful, like Irenaeus, Athanasius, and the Cappadocians, whose teachings were within the limits outlined in the councils. After conciliar decisions, a great temptation persisted through the centuries to define orthodoxy as submission to the formularies and to forget that the creeds did not die for us upon the cross. Repeating in parrot-fashion the fruit of centuries of struggle, "three persons in the unity of one substance," could mean little more than asserting an absurdity. Since the plural of "person" is "people" and "substance" means to most twentieth-century ears "material," would this mean no more than that we worship "three people in the unity of one material?" Thus, orthodoxy must continually be reinterpreted and translated into contemporary meanings (or recapitulated, as perhaps Irenaeus would say), or it will become something even worse than heresy, that is, idolatry. One primary purpose of this book is to express, in today's terms, the meaning and relevance of Christian orthodoxy.

6

Apollinarianism

Gabriel (to Mary)
When Eve, in love with her own will,
Denied the will of Love and fell
She turned the flesh Love knew so well
To knowledge of her love until
Both love and knowledge were of sin:
What her negation wounded, may
Your affirmation heal today;
Love's will requires your own, that in
The flesh whose love you do not know,
Love's knowledge into flesh may grow.
                              W. H. Auden[1]

The Council at Constantinople in 381 succeeded in establishing the church's teaching against a persistent Arianism, but it also dealt with Apollinarianism, a heresy from the opposite end of the spectrum. The condemnation of Apollinarius was especially tragic since he was among the most attractive and admirable of all heretics. He lived from about 315 to 390 and was bishop of Laodicea. Both he and his father were brilliant scholars and generous men. When the Emperor Julian, whose paganism was of intense proportions, decreed that no Christians would be allowed to give instruction in the classics, Apollinarius feared that the Christian church would be cut off from the intellectual life of the empire.

Realizing the harm this would do to the general education of Christians, Apollinarius, together with his father, reproduced the scriptures in classical form, rendering the early part of the Old Testament into an epic poem of twenty-four books, and the gospels into Platonic dialogues. In addition, they produced a number of tragedies and comedies in the style of Greek dramatists. This endeavor allowed Christians to keep in touch with classical culture even under the hostile imperial edict of Julian. Apollinarius also published a number of commentaries on various books of the Bible and over thirty volumes criticizing pagan philosophy. It is difficult to think of anyone in church history who did more to meet the educational needs of his time.

As a friend of Athanasius, Apollinarius was an ardent supporter of *homoousios* and was instrumental in the defeat of the Arians. With all these laudable assets, why was his teaching considered heretical? Apollinarius represents the Alexandrian concern to emphasize the unity with God in the act of salvation and the necessity of Christ's divinity to accomplish it. Thus he was immensely helpful in combating that Antiochene aspect of Arius' teaching which denied Christ's oneness with the Father.

However, the full humanity of Jesus was insufficiently appreciated in Alexandria and the Antiochene emphasis on the fully human Jesus recorded in scripture was overlooked. A real problem lay beneath the tensions of these two cities and their hold on their respective values. As we have noticed, heresies are never completely false. Much of their strength is derived from the truth they contain. The church must ever beware, in victory over a heresy such as Arianism, lest it lose something essential in its reaction.

When we worship Christ we firmly assert that we are worshiping "very God of very God . . . of one substance with the Father." But with this, a real problem arises. The trinitarian solution leads us to a christological problem: How is the divine logos related to the man Jesus? How is Christ also God? Or, to put it another way, if the Son is fully God, how is he related to the humanness in the man Jesus?

Apollinarius knew that Christ was not two persons but one. He saw the union of God and humanity in the one person of Christ as accomplished by the divine logos replacing the mind (*nous*) of Christ. Thus Jesus possessed a human body but not a human mind. This solution resolved the distinctions of humanity and divinity by asserting a unity that in effect destroyed something of the humanity. The Alexandrian virtue of unity and its weakness regarding humanity resulted in a Sabellian "solution," the sacrifice of the everlasting manifestation of God as Christ and Spirit. Apollinarianism's virtue was the establishment of unity in the person of Christ but at the sacrifice of his full humanity. Apollinarianism is to Christology as Sabellianism is to the Trinity; each sacrifices the distinctions in its affirmation of the unity.

Apollinarianism also violated the everlastingly valuable Cappadocian axiom: "What he (Christ) did not assume he could not redeem."[2] The soteriological question, "How can humanity be saved?", that helped to explain the difference between Arius and Athanasius exposes the ultimate cruelty of Apollinarius' teaching: we are "saved" by "replacement," by destruction. The humanity of Christ is one with God, but not with all of his humanity. Whereas there were two natures, divine and human, before the incarnation, afterward there is only a divine nature. The mind of Jesus was replaced and therefore lost.[3] This heresy is also termed "Monophysite" as teaching one (*mono*) nature (*physis*). As orthodoxy saw the necessity of Christ's full divinity to have the power to redeem, at the same time it saw the necessity of Jesus' complete human nature for the redeeming power to be transmitted to mankind.

The pastoral and practical implications of this teaching are shown in such remarks as, "I liked him better before he was converted." Something human was perceived to have been lost when someone became a Christian. Much of conventional Christianity today is Apollinarian. "Don't ask questions, just have faith," as if one's mind must be left outside church. "They built the door to the church so low you can't get your head in." Christianity does not teach that one's mind must be replaced in the process of salvation. Much of the appeal of cults has been, and still is, that they offer to turn our minds off (or over to a group or guru). Never having to use one's mind to think, to question, or to decide makes Apollinarian solutions perennially attractive.

Peter's Epistle assures us to the contrary that our minds are very much a part of our redemption: "Always be prepared to make a defense to anyone who calls you to account for the hope that is in you" *(1 Pet. 3:15)*. Paul also makes it clear that salvation enlightens rather than diminishes or destroys reason. "I appeal to you . . . to present your bodies as a living sacrifice, . . . which is your spiritual worship . . . be transformed by the renewal of your mind" *(Rom. 12:1-2)*.

Apollinarius taught that human will is located in the mind *(nous)*; therefore the human will is replaced or destroyed in the process of salvation. We can see modern examples of similar "solutions" to the problem of being human in B.F. Skinner's *Beyond Freedom and Dignity* and in certain behavioral therapies that seek to train, educate, or cure people with methods and techniques that circumvent or destroy the will. On a broader level the Apollinarian "solution" is a corollary of all tyranny. Giving up anxiety, which invariably accompanies freedom, in order to be cured, saved, unified, or "to have the trains run on time," has had lasting appeal in all ages.

Anthony Burgess' book and movie *A Clockwork Orange* is an example of the appeal and horror of this solution, the destruction of the will to resolve the problem of being human. Erich Fromm's book *Escape From Freedom* discloses the psychological dynamic in human nature that makes us praise our freedom and, at the same time, run away from it or willingly give it up.

Thus, Apollinarianism is an example of a subtle Docetism that sacrifices the full incarnate humanity of Christ and abets our desire to flee the implications of full human involvement. The Platonic and Alexandrian tendency to describe God in such terms as "impassible" and "immutable" without the balance of the passion of our Lord encouraged Apollinarius' teaching. It led him to insist that the divine logos, which becomes the mind of Christ, is immutable (*atreptos*). This resulting picture of Jesus is at complete odds with that of scripture.

If Christ's mind and will were immutable, it would render the temptations meaningless. How could he have been tempted if his will were unchangeable? It is recorded that he "increased in wisdom and in stature" (*Luke 2:52*) and that "although he was a Son, he learned obedience through what he suffered" (*Heb. 5:8*). The Gethsemane scene depicts the opposite of such superhuman attributes of impassibility and immutability, showing Jesus praying in agony, "Father, if thou art willing, remove this cup from me; nevertheless not my will, but thine, be done" (*Lk. 22:42*). The passion of the crucifixion portrayed in all four gospels contrasts starkly with the Apollinarian implication that only the body could be capable of suffering, or that Jesus did not possess a human will and a fully human nature.

Unless the incarnation involves the whole person, that which is replaced or left out does not become part of the salvation package. The neatness gained in the face of a real problem—how can the divine and human be united in Christ—was purchased at too great a price. Apollinarius excluded from salvation that whole aspect of fallen human nature which involves pride, self-will and those dangerous sins that Dante set in purgatory closest to hell. An experienced pastor can testify that the most difficult problems he deals with are those that arise from the soul and intellect rather than those from the body and its appetites. These latter are more often symptoms and expressions of the former "spiritual sins" than of mere appetite.

Gnostic dualism that sees flesh as bad and soul as good tends to blind the eyes of those who favor Apollinarianism. The word "flesh" in Paul's epistles refers to the whole of life under the dominion of sin and death. Our souls and fallen human spirits are as much in need of redemption as our flesh. The failure to acknowledge this inevitably leads to a concern for symptoms rather than the deeper root of sin.

A very perceptive physician once described how he had changed his approach to the treatment of dyshydrosis, a problem of unusual sweating and blisters in the hands. This is frequently a symptom of undue stress and was traditionally treated by bandaging both hands for several days, a most inconvenient and frustrating period of time for the patient.

Today, however, with the modern drug cortisone, the condition can be cleared up rapidly with application and no bandaging. The patient need not be inconvenienced and can go on with his or her normal schedule. Yet this doctor says that, in treating some cases, he does not use cortisone. He goes back to the traditional bandaged hands and inconvenient frustration for the patient. Why? Cortisone, he explained, was so effective in eliminating the symptom of serious stress on the body that patients were deprived of the warning implicit in the discomfort. In effect, cortisone treatment was turning off the alarm without dealing with the fire, whereas the inconvenience of the bandage treatment would perhaps make the patient more likely to deal with the underlying condition in order to avoid the inconvenience of further and more serious eruptions.

This doctor may not have known the technical meaning of Apollinarianism but he certainly understood the human dynamic that continues to make Apollinarianism attractive. In certain situations, cortisone could be called an Apollinarian prescription. "Fix my skin, Doctor, but don't ask me to change the way I live," parallels the Apollinarian "Save my body but leave the rest of me alone."

While not as gross as the Docetic complete denial of Jesus' physical existence or his suffering, Apollinarianism limits the humanity to the physical and excludes soul and psyche from redemptive suffering. It thus treats only the symptoms of sin while neglecting its deeper roots. The body becomes a scapegoat, as it does also in Manichaeism.

St. Augustine has taught that we cannot be saved *by* our wills, but that God will not save us *without* our wills. That we are saved by our wills is the Pelagian mistake (which we shall meet in the next chapter). That God will save us without our wills is the Apollinarian mistake.

The latter is far more attractive, for it seems to offer the hope of health and salvation without effort, pain, or struggle. It is like answering an advertisement that promises to teach you a foreign language while you sleep. Apollinarianism can be a basic dynamic in magic.

Holy things and holy places have a dangerous tendency to be used magically. That which is sacred has its sacred power not by God's divine action alone but also in God's action through human response (we must not forget that faith itself is a gift of God). When a people who have experienced a holy place, a Bethel, and a holy meal, a Eucharist, cease to give to subsequent generations the vision that enables them to see the place and the meal as holy, these cease to have the power of holiness for those descendants.

Paul Tillich insists that:

> it is important to draw the boundary line between the impact of a sacrament on the conscious through the unconscious self (on the one hand) and the magical techniques which influence the unconscious without the consent of the will (on the other) . . . But if it is exercised as a particular intentional act—bypassing the personal—it is a demonic distortion. And every sacrament is in danger of becoming demonic.[4]

We shall know the truth only as we continue as Christ's disciples (*John 8:32*). Those whose wills led them to follow Barabbas were unable to discern the presence of the Messiah. Those whose wills led them to follow Christ could see "My Lord and my God" in Jesus. One can see the providence of God in the events of history only as one has been given the will to see. Helen Keller, who was without the faculty of sight, could discern the things of the Spirit with the "eyes" of her will. The Apollinarian teaching that the human mind and will were not assumed but replaced in the incarnation omitted the very human faculty which, when transformed, perceives and knows the things of God.

The Cappadocian wisdom that "what he did not assume he does not redeem" is paralleled by another axiom: "Grace never destroys nature." Deeper than Marx's claim that workers "have nothing to lose but their chains" is the Christian promise that we have "nothing to lose but our sin." Nothing that is truly human is lost in redemption. Death in baptism is *to* self, not *of* self. He came that we "may have life, and have it more abundantly" (*John 10:10*) and that your "joy may be full" (*John 16:24*).

Replacement, in Apollinarian redemption, is destruction, but it appeals to that part of human nature that tempted the children of Israel to return to slavery in Egypt, that resists its own salvation ("He came to his own home and his own people received him not" *John 1:11*), that prefers to flee rather than to fight and would rather die than change ("I have no pleasure in the death of the wicked, but that the wicked turn from their ways and live" *Ezek. 33:11 NRSV*). Apollinarianism attempts to resolve a real problem, yet in effect it is but a less obvious and more subtle version of earlier Docetism. Apollinarianism carries with it the whole baggage of Docetic implications for all who would "bow the knee" in worship before the Apollinarian Christ. His insistence that Christ had only a divine nature led him to deny explicitly that Christ was a man: " . . . whoever calls him Who was born of Mary a man, and calls him who was crucified a human, makes him a man instead of God."[5]

This either/or approach, which is characteristic of all, ancient and modern, who recoil from the ambiguities of historical existence, needs to be corrected by that balancing Antiochene thought whose virtue was to take the history and data of scripture with utmost seriousness. One such theologian, who insisted that only as Christ became what we human beings are did he reunite us with God, was Theodore of Mopsuestia (ca. 350-428).

> If he had not assumed a human soul, and it were only the deity that won the victory, then that which happened would bring us no gain, for what similarity is there between the perfection of the conduct of God and that human soul? . . . He took flesh and soul, and fought by both for both, in that he slew sin in the flesh and diminished its lusts, . . . but the soul he instructed and trained to overcome its passions as well as to bridle the lusts of the flesh.[6]

Any teaching that asserts salvation as divinely imposed on the human predicament is like a teacher who gives the answers without allowing the students to become agents in their own learning. It is like a parent whose love drives him to let the child win in all games, to protect the child from the bully, to do his son's homework, to arrange her daughter's marriage, to insulate and protect his or her children from temptation and suffering.

What physician is not tempted to give the prescription and to treat the symptoms mechanically and impersonally without taking the time to enlist the understanding and cooperation of the patient as an agent in his or her own health? Who among the clergy has not been tempted to "solve" pastoral problems *for* parishioners, or has not found in matters of counseling, administration, and worship that "it is easier to decide and to do it myself"? Anyone who watches citizens, clients, patients, parishioners, or children wreck their lives for lack of the right answers can feel the tug of an Apollinarian divinity who will save us by replacing our wills with proper directions, thereby sacrificing something essential of mature humanity.

In Martin Luther's "Table Talk," there is a story of family prayer that involved a discussion of the story of the sacrifice of Isaac by Abraham. His wife, Katie, speaking for all of us, exclaimed, "How horrible! God would not allow his son to be sacrificed!" And Luther quietly replied, "But, Katie, he did." The horror in the story is only partly relieved by the substitution of the ram for Isaac, and not at all relieved later by the absence of any intervention to bring Christ down from the cross. But beneath this horror is a love that is tough enough not to destroy humanity in order to save it, and a love powerful enough to see humanity vindicated over death.

Divine patience that insists on working through and thereby transforming humanity is not the whole story (there are times to intervene—on God's part and ours), but it is an essential part of it. The unwillingness of God to intervene prematurely, to save the Only Begotten from the betrayal, from the agony of the garden, and from the cry of dereliction and temptation to despair on the cross is the great challenge to our all-too-human desire for an Apollinarian short-cut.

A seminarian taking a summer's course on the oncology ward of a hospital was described by his supervisor as making the universal mistake of "giving premature reassurance." "Premature reassurance" is a kind of Apollinarian sentimentality that is long-range cruelty. Unfortunately, everyone does not always get well, and to suggest that they will does not provide for that patience which allows one to respond in trust to whatever reality obtains. We need to make room for a deeper hope than the one we pray for at a given time.

A New York jazz pianist once observed, "God never comes when you want him, but he's right on time." All of us caught in the agonies of God's failure to come on our schedule become especially susceptible to the seduction of the Apollinarian hope that we will be saved without being changed, without our wills being changed through the painful stretching of our time into God's.

The Creed of Nicaea and Constantinople

Against	Text
	I believe in one God,
Gnosticism	the Father Almighty,
and	maker of heaven and earth,
Marcionism	and of all things visible and invisible;
	And in one Lord Jesus Christ,
	the only-begotten Son of God,
Adoptionism	begotten of his Father before all worlds,
	God of God, Light of Light,
Arianism	very God of very God,
	begotten, not made,
	being of one substance with the Father;
	by whom all things were made;
	who for us men and for our salvation
	came down from heaven,
Adoptionism	and was incarnate by the Holy Ghost of the Virgin Mary,
Apollinarianism	and was made man;
Docetism	and was crucified also for us under Pontius Pilate;
	he suffered and was buried;
	and the third day he rose again according to the Scriptures,
	and ascended into heaven,
	and sitteth on the right hand of the Father;
Sabellianism	and he shall come again, with glory,
	to judge both the quick and the dead;
	whose kingdom shall have no end.
Macedonianism	And I believe in the Holy Ghost the Lord,
(Holy Spirit was	and Giver of Life
created, not equal	who proceedeth from the Father;[7]
person of Trinity)	who with the Father and the Son together is worshiped and glorified;
Marcionism	who spake by the Prophets.
	And I believe one holy Catholic and Apostolic Church;
Donatism	I acknowledge one Baptism for the remission of sins;
	and I look for the resurrection of the dead,
	and the life of the world to come.

There is more than enough to repel us as we look at the surface of the historical events in which theological issues of the Christian faith were hammered out in a context of personal animosities, political intrigue, and patriarchal rivalries among the participants of synods and councils. Hilary of Poitiers (ca. 315-67) writes:

> Since the Nicene Council we have done nothing but write the creed. While we fight about words, inquire about novelties, take advantage of ambiguities, criticise authors, fight on party questions, have difficulties in agreeing, and prepare to anathematize one another, there is scarcely a man who belongs to Christ.[8]

Yet, accurate as this assessment is, beneath the surface is the life and work of St. Hilary himself which discloses a depth of faith and commitment that marks him as Christ's own. Hilary, Irenaeus, Athanasius, and the Cappadocian Fathers, all leaders of the church, were scarcely given time between councils and conferences to say their prayers or to learn their own minds, but behind them and visible to us only through them was a great mass of simple, suffering, serving, living and loving Christians. These leaders were but the organs and instruments produced, supported, and sustained by a holy folk whose general theological and philosophical naivete is not to be confused with superficial piety.

After a long appreciation of the three great fourth-century theologians, the Cappadocians, Dr. DuBose writes:

> remember that there must have been a soil out of which such men grew, and but learn the names of the mothers and sisters and friends at home who nurtured and influenced and stimulated and encouraged them,—and however one may blush or smile at the abundant folly and weakness that appears upon the surface, it will be impossible to doubt or ignore the continuous presence and grace of God and the living power of Christianity in the church. There is abundant proof in contemporary literature that while the bishops were being swayed here and there by

political and worldly considerations; or, what was much more common, by their own indecision, and vacillation with regard to issues and questions upon which they were compelled and yet were not prepared to take sides; the great body of the faithful permitted to live in peace and leave thought and speculation alone were actually living lives of as deep and sincere Christian faith, devotion, and charity as have characterized any age of the church.[9]

7

Nestorianism:
The Train of Salvation
Does Not Stop for Sinners

Jesus said to the woman taken in adultery, "Has no
one condemned you?" She said, "No one, Lord."
And Jesus said, "Neither do I condemn you; go,
and do not sin again."

John 8:10-11

We have seen a pendulum swing between the Docetic and
Adoptionist heresies, between the opposing tendencies of Alexandria and Antioch. The Arian thought of Antioch helped defeat
Sabellianism at the Synod of Antioch in 269. Apollinarius and
his school helped defeat the Arianism that persisted after the
Council of Nicaea. The Antiochenes, such as Theodore of
Mopsuestia, helped defeat the Apollinarians at Constantinople
in 381. It should be no surprise that the next heresy came from
Antioch. Both Alexandria and Antioch loyally accepted the
decision of the Second General Council that, in the incarnation, God was united with a full and perfect humanity. Yet the
question that Apollinarius had tried to answer still remained:
How is this union effected?

Theodore of Mopsuestia (350-428), born and raised in Antioch,
represented both the strengths and weaknesses of the Antiochene school. His faithfulness to the New Testament portrait of

Jesus, and the consequent insistence upon the full humanity of Christ, were characteristically orthodox Antiochene teaching. The Adoptionist tendency remained but was tempered and domesticated into more subtle manifestations over the centuries. After the Council of Constantinople neither the full divinity nor the full humanity of Christ was denied as had been the case with earlier Arianism and the even earlier teaching of Paul of Samosata (Bishop of Antioch ca. 260-70).

Paul had taught that Jesus was not divine by nature but became God by virtue. This "rough draft" of Nestorianism, though modified through successive decades, failed to provide a description of the Trinity or of Christ that lived up to its soteriological purpose, to bring God and humanity together in a saving relationship.

It is often supposed that the contrast between Alexandria and Antioch was that the former emphasized the divinity of Christ at the expense of his full humanity while the latter emphasized the humanity at the expense of the divinity. Unity, not divinity, was what suffered in Antioch. Arius affirmed a divinity of Christ (albeit a lesser one), and Paul of Samosata, Theodore of Mopsuestia, and Nestorius (all three theologians whose teachings were to be condemned as "Nestorian") asserted both the humanity and the divinity of Christ but were accused of denying the unity.

This is an important point because the widespread denial of Christ's divinity in modern times finds no reflection in any of the major classical heresies. One must go back to the very beginning of Christianity to find the primitive heresy that denied Christ's divinity, Psilanthropism. It was so rare that one must be something of a specialist even to have heard of it.

What saved the Antiochene school from ever settling for a merely human Jesus was their commitment to the Old Testament, in which the pilgrimage of God's people was worked out on such a profound level that they knew that only some agency of divine proportions could save Israel. (This commitment is frequently absent among modern Adoptionists.)

Theodore precipitated a debate in the fifth century by insisting that the union of the divine logos and the humanity of Jesus was not essential (*ousios*), only moral. This union was not of being but of behavior, a union of good will, in that the fully human Jesus obeyed the will of the fully divine logos. The resulting "unity" appeared to be either two persons or a contrived and theoretical third entity. Things came to a head when Theodore objected to calling the Virgin Mary by the term *theotokos,* meaning "bearer of God." (Later it came to mean "mother of God," but this has nothing to do with the quite different issues regarding the virgin birth or even the much later teaching of the Immaculate Conception.) This term concerns Jesus Christ in regard to the unity of his divinity and humanity. Nestorius (died ca. 451), a famous preacher, an abbot of Antioch and later Patriarch of Constantinople, agreed with Theodore in objecting to the term *theotokos.* He preferred the title "mother of Christ," although he saw the possible danger of transferring worship of Christ to his mother in popular piety. His main fear was that the term *theotokos* might lead Christians to believe that "God was born."

Nestorius accepted that the full humanity of Christ but not the divine logos was born of Mary. His critics objected that he had so separated the two natures that the result was not an essential union, not a single person. Nestorius' choice of *prosopon* (person) to describe both the divine and human nature (*physis*) made it seem even more likely that Christ was two persons.

Weighty evidence has caused modern scholars to raise serious questions as to whether Nestorius was himself actually Nestorian. It is true that his rival, Cyril of Alexandria, was motivated more by rivalry and jealousy over the rising influence of Constantinople than by theological issues. Certainly Cyril, with his persistent Alexandrian Apollinarianism, did not deserve to be regarded as "orthodox" as he appeared.

It is enough for our purposes to acknowledge that, as usual, many non-theological and non-scriptural issues played large roles in the Third General Council of Ephesus in 431 and that the repudiation of some of Nestorius' teachings were not only unfair but continue to cause theological difficulties today. However, we are concerned to understand Nestorianism and can leave Nestorius himself to the kinder judgment of God.

Nestorianism can best be described by an illustration comparing it with Arianism and Apollinarianism.

Arianism: Created, lesser deity
not of the same substance (essence)

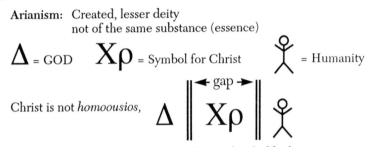

Christ is not *homoousios*,

but only *homoiousios: like* the Father and only *like* human nature. There is no *At-one-ment,* no substantial identification with God or humanity, no union of God and humanity in Christ—no salvation.

Nicaea 325:

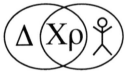

homoousios with Father
and with humanity

Atonement of God and humanity in Christ. Christ *homoousios* with the Father and with humanity

Condemned Arianism

Apollinarianism: Christ fully divine,
not fully human

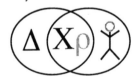

Leaves out the mind (soul) from scheme of redemption.

Redemption is by replacement or destruction of something human

Constantinople 381: Reasserted Nicaean Victory over Arianism
and affirmed full human nature against
Apollinarianism.

Nestorianism: Christ is fully divine
and fully human but two persons
joined in unity by will

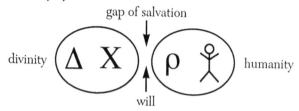

gap of salvation

divinity   humanity

will

Christ possesses not
just two *natures (physis)*
but two *persons (prosopon)*
with the unity dependent
upon the moral agreement
of the two wills.

The unity of salvation is only that unity
of the will. As Jesus and the logos
are one by their wills, so we will be one
with Christ as long as our wills are
his will. No unity, no ontology (being)
but only unity by will-power.

Ephesus 431:

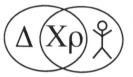

One person-true atonement
Two natures

Nestorianism has improved on Arianism in that it asserts the
full divinity and full humanity of Jesus Christ. The two fatal Arian
gaps between God and Christ and between Christ and humanity are now reduced to one, and that in Christ himself. Thus,
Nestorianism denies not divinity but rather the soteriological
unity by which God and humanity are one in Christ.

The place of *theotokos* then can be seen in its affirmation
that the logos and Christ are essentially and ontologically one
person (in his very being), not just in "their" congruity of will,
ethics, and morals. *Theotokos* (God-bearer), implying essential
union (ontological from conception), would not allow for any
interpretation of Jesus' baptism as the conferring of divinity (as
we have seen in Adoptionism). *Theotokos,* no matter how it is
later used, did establish the unity of one person from conception.

The Council of Ephesus resolved the problem by using the
word "nature" (*physis*) for the divine and human aspects in

Christ and "person" (*prosopon*) for the single unity of divinity and humanity. Thus we have in Christ two natures (as against the Apollinarian one nature) and one person (as over against the Nestorian two persons).

The key to understanding this Council is its orthodox desire to preserve the function of salvation in the incarnation. It is like going to the station to board a train, but finding that the Apollinarian train carries only freight and not people, while the Nestorian train comes through the station but does not stop. Nestorian insistence on the humanity tells us that it is the right station and the train does come through but only at full speed. Its one connection with us is the example that the human Jesus ran fast enough to catch the divine logos and so should we. We can catch the train of salvation as long as we have made our wills the will of Jesus as his will is the Father's will.

What separates the orthodox from Nestorians are such scriptural texts as "By his wounds you have been healed" *(Isa. 53:5)*, *(1 Pet. 2:24)*; "For our sake he made him to be sin, who knew no sin so that in him we might become the righteousness of God" *(2 Cor. 5:21)*. Somehow, Christ's saving accessibility to sinners must be preserved for us to get on board. In Christ, God's train stops at our town even if its very name is Sin. In this context we can imagine a rough analogy that may help us to understand the mystery of how sinful human nature is redeemed by the suffering of Christ on the cross.

Boatmen use a trick to solve a very difficult problem that water causes when it gets in a gas tank and fouls the motor. Going through the carburetor into the cylinder, water prevents spark plugs from firing and the engine stops. All is not lost, however, if one has a couple of cans of denatured alcohol on board. Alcohol has a property that gasoline lacks. It will mix with water and it will burn. So pouring alcohol, which absorbs water, into the tank and cranking the engine enough to get the alcohol sucked into the spark plug chamber will start the motor and remove the water from the gas tank. As alcohol absorbs water and burns it in the motor, so Christ's humanity absorbs human sin and burns it on the cross. Divinity cannot absorb sin any more than gasoline can absorb water. For sin to be absorbed and destroyed it requires a humanity that can carry it. ("For our sake he made him to be sin . . . that we might become the righteousness of God.")

This is why the claim of the seventeenth-century Anglican bishop Jeremy Taylor, that "[when] the will loves it [lust], . . . God cannot love the man: for God is the prince of purities, and the Son of God is the King of Virgins,"[1] is Nestorian. But in prayers such as the following, Taylor is thoroughly orthodox:

> I know that a thousand years of tears and sorrow, the purity of angels, the love of saints, and the humiliation of the greatest penitent, is not sufficient to make me worthy to dwell with thee, to be united to thy infinity, to be fed with thy body and refreshed with thy purest blood, to become bone of thy bone, and flesh of thy flesh, and spirit of thy spirit. . . . But what I cannot be of myself, let me be made by thee.[2]

The cruelty involved in Nestorianism is the persistent one that belongs to Adoptionism, that the salvation promised in the work of Christ is reduced to the imperative to be like him. According to this heresy, as Jesus is one with the logos by his will, we are one with Christ by our wills. This crucial emphasis upon the will to make Nestorianism work brought in a twin heresy, Pelagianism.

Pelagianism teaches that the human will has the power to break the bondage of sin. It is best understood as a theological synonym for "nagging," or confidence that the law requires no more than humans can do. When Jesus says, "Be ye perfect . . ." *(Matt. 5:48)*, we simply must get busy doing it. Therefore, Pelagian Christianity is characterized by exhortation and scolding. Confidence in the power of human will leads to confidence that the defeat of sin can be effected by means of fear.

The Whole Duty of Man, an anonymous work of the seventeenth century, poured this Nestorian/Pelagian poison into the English-speaking world as the single most popular devotional writing for two hundred years. The purpose of preaching, it claimed, is merely to remind us of our duties. Morals are nineteen of the twenty parts of religion. All the threats of wrath, punishment, miseries both temporal and spiritual, and everlasting destruction in the life to come, we "are most steadfastly to believe, that these are God's threats."[3]

Sinners should be made to "apprehend their damnation and to grasp its nearness."[4] The underlying confidence in the power of the human will to make one sinless is Pelagian. The requirement for sinlessness to come to Holy Communion, to be forgiven, or to be in Christ is based on the ancient Nestorian Christology that makes us one with Christ as long as we have made our wills the same as his. We must have on the "wedding garment" that is our own righteousness before we come to the Feast. Forgiveness of any sin is promised only to him who "forsaketh it." "Nothing but an entire forsaking of every evil" is the condition for pardon.[5]

It is significant that the eighteenth-century philosopher David Hume writes of being put off quite early in life by reading *The Whole Duty of Man*. Hume regretted on his death-bed that he was leaving unfinished "the great work" of liberating Scotland "from the Christian superstition."[6] Hume's departure from Christianity is a complicated matter. Too few philosophers and historians have noted the understandable reaction, not to orthodoxy but to Hume's mistaking a cruelly oppressive heresy as orthodox Christianity.[6]

The sentiments expressed in *The Whole Duty of Man* contrast starkly with the deeper perceptions of that earlier Anglican, Richard Hooker: "Howbeit, when faith hath wrought a fear of the event of sin, yet repentance hereupon ensueth not, unless our belief conceive both the possibility and the means to avert evil." We cannot "possibly forsake sin unless we first begin again to love. . . . I therefore conclude, that fear worketh no man's inclination to repentance, till somewhat else have wrought in us love also."[7]

The cruelty implicit in reducing the gospel to nagging is the despair it produces. Insensitivity to the profound bondage of human beings to sin is characteristic of the Nestorian teaching about Christ and the Pelagian teaching of will power. *The Whole Duty of Man* is not the only example of several centuries of popular teaching and preaching, crossing denominational lines, that required sinlessness as a condition of pardon. However, Archbishop Thomas Cranmer's absolution prayer in the *Book of Common Prayer* discloses a much deeper appreciation of the human condition and the need of forgiveness in order to repent more fully.

> The almighty and merciful Lord grant you absolution and remission of all your sins, true repentance, amendment of life, and the grace and consolation of his Holy Spirit. Amen

Note that "true repentance" follows the grace of absolution, a sequence unknown to the Antiochene tradition, with its literalistic and superficial view of scripture, history, and the dynamics of grace. It is clear that there is a *chronology* of repentance before forgiveness, but there is a necessary and deeper *kairology* (from *kairos,* "God's time" in contrast to *kronos,* simple "clock time") in the relationship between repentance and forgiveness, forgiveness and repentance. Surely the Prodigal Son's singularly unworthy repentance in the pig-pen is exceeded by his repentance after his father's gracious reception *(Luke 15:11-32).*

The Nestorian heresy attempted to explain how Christ is both divine and human. In doing so, it unfortunately set up a barrier to human salvation. The Nestorians proposed a unity of Christ's divinity and his humanity that was merely moral in nature. Their construction has the appearance of logic and consistency but, in fact, brings us to the decisive issue of Christ's humanity where we either get on board or miss the train altogether.

If Christ's humanity is one with his divinity merely by the

moral agreement of the human and the divine wills, our oneness with Christ is likewise founded on the moral basis of our
wills being the will of Christ. We are left with a hope of unity in
Christ founded not on God's act in our baptism, but on our own
wills, which is no hope at all. Whatever else is wrong with
Nestorianism, it simply does not work.

It is like the story of a boy who broke his father's favorite
canoe paddle. Without telling his father, the boy applied car-
penter's white glue to the break, put it in a vise overnight, and
presented it the next day as "good as new." It was indeed so
strongly mended that, if broken again, it would likely break some-
where else. What the son did not know was that the white glue
was water soluble. As soon as the paddle was put in water it came
apart.

So it is with Nestorianism. As long as this union of divine and
human natures is cemented by the will alone, it may seem to
work well in theory but in the real world of sinful human
beings, unable to make our wills one with Christ's will, our
unity with him comes unglued. Nestorianism is "sin soluble."
The unity promised by Nestorianism is continually dissolved by
sin. Christianity did not and cannot start with people who have
forsaken sin. It receives them and begins to free them from the
bondage that is sin.

"Let this mind be in you which is also in Christ Jesus" (Phil.
2:5) is an exhortation to Christians, not a requirement for keep-
ing our membership in the Christian family. Nestorianism is
like a couple telling an adopted child, "Your relationship with
us is based on your obedience to us. As long as you do as you're
told, you can be a member of this family." A social worker in an
adoption agency, we would hope, would recognize this attitude
as one unfit for rearing a child.

Nestorians can be divided into "hard" Nestorians and "soft"
Nestorians. The former have no compassion for sinners and we
are either excluded from the fellowship or we must live by
hypocrisy. The latter tell us, that if we lack the freedom to stop

sinning, then it must not be sin after all. This could be called "salvation by redefinition."

The Council of Ephesus insisted upon "ontological" union as opposed to the mere "moral" union of Nestorianism. Ontology is a difficult concept for the modern mind to grasp, but it is crucial to our understanding if we are to avoid the cruelty of moralism. Ontological union is like being in and belonging to a family on a deeper level than that of behavior. Behavior is not unimportant, but one is enabled to behave as one senses the confidence of this belonging, this *being* in Christ.

Parents who adopt a child, ontologically—that is the child belongs to that family in its very being—are providing the indispensable union of parents and child. This being and belonging is necessary for the child to fulfill the appropriate expectations as a member of the family. "Mommy will love you when you quit wetting your diapers" is Nestorian toilet training.

Nestorianism continues to thrive, not merely because we are influenced by the Antiochene tradition, but also because we tend to seek a religious solution to the problem of being human that does not require a death to our self-centered self. Like Nicodemus, only at night do we usually come to the question, "How can these things be?" *(John 3:9)*, when told by Jesus that we must be born again in him and not continue our self-centered ways.

"By myself!" is the universal cry of children at a certain age. We must all go through this stage before we become mature enough to share dependent love, but it is symptomatic of the tenacious human drive to be independent of God as well as of others. We have seen this infantile aversion to mature, loving dependence in the Arian insistence that the dependent servanthood of Christ is the mark of an inferior deity. Mature dependency in no way denies equality. Instead it is a mark of deepest love.

Humility, which is required to discern the profound dignity in servanthood, characterizes not only the shocking quality of

Christ's ministry *(Phil. 2:7)*, but is the essence of all Christian ministry *(diakanos*—a minister, a servant). To be a part of him and his ministry, the shell around our self's center must be broken that we might be brought to that agonizing capitulation. "Not my will but thine be done," and be born again with a new center, Jesus Christ.

Will and Freedom

Nestorianism and Pelagianism operate on the assumption that freedom is having one's will. A young man quit graduate school because a sudden inheritance made him "free" from the stress of having to earn a degree. His subsequent affluent aimlessness, he realized too late, was more bondage than freedom. He learned what Augustine and Luther understood but Pelagius and Erasmus did not: that the power to implement one's will could be bondage, not freedom. Money often means power. To be given power is freedom if our wills are God's wills. But if our wills are self-indulgent and self-centered, power results not in freedom but in greater bondage.

The popular conviction that freedom means being able to choose what one wants is shown to be false by Dante's *Divine Comedy,* in which people are in the bondage of hell by being given precisely what their wills desired. Only when our wills are changed into God's will can our wills be free. To the extent that a person's self-centered will is implemented, it is in bondage, not freedom. We can see this more easily in others than in ourselves. Intelligence and scholarship do not rectify this malady of the heart since the same self-centered will is at the root of the problem. Jesus said to those Jews

> who had believed in him, "If you continue in my word, you are truly my disciples, and you will know the truth, and the truth will make you free." They answered him, "We are descendants of Abraham, and have never been in bondage to anyone. How is it that you say, 'You will be made free'?" *(John 8:31-33).*

It is important to notice that this early form of Pelagianism occurred even among the Jews who "believed in him." The fact that it is an error of the heart and not of the head is revealed by how proudly they could recall being "children of Abraham" while, at the same time, denying that they were freed by Moses from *slavery* in Egypt, a more recent event that was religiously recalled each year at the Passover.

Instead of pointing out this obvious fact to them, Jesus goes deeper into the matter and reminds them that sin itself is bondage ("everyone who commits sin is a slave of sin"—v. 34), and that true freedom is possible only if the Son makes us free (then we will "be free indeed"—v. 36) It seems to be a condition of our human nature that we continue the denial shown by the Jews "who believed in him." This denial seeks to preserve the vain hope that we shall be free by having our wills fulfilled without the radical change that they need.

We have heard sin and freedom used as synonyms: free to get drunk, free to steal, free to commit suicide, when the opposite is true. These are conditions of bondage. Samuel Taylor Coleridge saw this assumption of freedom in the initial situation as flattering to our presumed autonomy but in actuality such a teaching is a "wolf in lamb's clothing."[8] You are truly free only when the "son makes you free," when our wills are made one with God's. From the time of Adam's apple to the "Jews who believe on him," to our present day, humans tenaciously believe that freedom means to have what we want. If what we want, and get, is also what God wants for us we will know a measure of freedom.

In fact, nowhere does the New Testament ever equate sin with freedom. On the contrary, the gospel equates sin with bondage, a bondage that is broken by the Word. We are promised that when we continue in God's Word we will be disciples, know the truth, and *then* be made free. Freedom is not assumed at the outset but is a result of the Word, discipleship and truth.

Some claim that Shakespeare said "to thine own self be true," but they forget that Shakespeare put this speech in the mouth of that silly old man, Polonius. The Polonius lie is the Nestorian hope to keep our self as center. Freedom is not found in the service of self but of Christ, in "whose service is perfect freedom" (Collect for Peace, *Book of Common Prayer,* 1979, p. 57). The comic strip character Pogo enunciated a profound truth: "We have met the enemy . . . and he is us." As long as we assume that freedom is having our desires fulfilled, the minds of infants and theologians alike will be skewed until and unless the self's own center is relinquished. Such a person to whom this happened was Augustine of Hippo (354-430).

Augustine of Hippo

Although he died in the year before the Third General Council of Ephesus in 431, Augustine's criticisms of Pelagius have become invaluable to any understanding of the inadequacy and cruelty of Nestorianism. We have seen how the Nestorian vision of Christ fits the Pelagian vision of human nature. Whatever injustice has been done in history to the man Nestorius, it must be admitted that both he and Theodore of Mopsuestia backed the teaching of Pelagianism, which is logically and ineluctably connected with a view of Christ that carries all the corroding acids of Nestorianism.

Augustine was distinguished by his superior intelligence, but the advantage he had over other theologians was the timing and radical nature of his conversion. The problem of freedom stems not from the intellect but from the very self. Humans, by themselves, can not see where their true freedom lies. It is like trying to repair one's eyeglasses when one needs the glasses to see to fix them. Augustine's intellect was the same when he was a Manichaean for nine years as later when he became a Christian. His conversion committed him to another center from whence his incomparable wisdom flowed.

Augustine himself tells us of his conversion. It was long in coming, despite the ceaseless prayers of his mother, Monica. He had been a Manichaean "hearer" and had studied rhetoric under the saintly Bishop Ambrose. But when he heard a child's voice saying "take up and read," he took it as a divine command and picked up his Bible, opening it to Romans 13:14. Sobbing deeply, he read the passage culminating in: "But put on the Lord Jesus Christ, and make no provision for the flesh, to gratify its desires."

To read his account is to see a painful transition from self as center to Christ as center. This transition, never an absolute victory in this life, is an experience to which we come in quite different ways. But it is an experience that one must have, in some measure, to understand what the New Testament means by freedom in Christ, something Nestorians and Pelagians do not understand no matter how clever they are.

At the heart of Augustine's argument against Pelagians is what one might call the "Augustinian conundrum":

Is it better

To be able not to sin or
Not to be able to sin?

In Latin it is

posse non peccare or
non posse peccare?

The puzzle divides Nestorians from Apollinarians. The latter would opt for "not able to sin." The divine logos having replaced the human mind of Jesus, he could not sin.

On the other hand, if we understand Christ as one who was "able not to sin," we envisage a "teeth-gritting" figure that is the hallmark of all versions of Adoptionism, such as Nestorianism. When one sees the epitome of freedom in Christ as a finally achieved "ability not to sin," the view is seen through Nestorian glasses. Since Christ controlled the will to sin, so must we. A "white-knuckle" religion of control becomes a "hopeful" vision of success.

Augustine insists that it is better "not to be able to sin," and he puts it in a non-Apollinarian way: Christ is "not able to sin," not because of a physical inability but a moral inability. Jesus was tempted in all things as we are but without sin *(Heb. 4:15)*. Obviously he was not tempted in each particular as we are. He was not tempted to tell the second lie since he had not told the first one. The Nestorians paint an unfortunate picture of freedom in which Jesus must control his passions of anger, lust, desire for revenge, and so forth. Most people enjoy a certain measure of freedom in not even being tempted by bizarre compulsions which beset some.

A "moral inability" to sin can be illustrated by the story of a lonely widow who once stole an entire rock garden from her neighbor. The widow had struggled for years against a rare form of kleptomania with little success. Certainly a vision of freedom for us is not that we will be able to resist and finally control the urge to steal a rock garden, but that we will be so free from that temptation that we could not morally do it. This "blessed liberty" is not a physical inability but a moral inability, a freedom from the desire.

Would one prefer to have a spouse who was "not able" to chop one in the head with a hatchet or one who was "able" not to do such a thing? "Well, we've gotten through one more day in which he was able not to wield the hatchet" is a considerably less desirable state than the confidence that he is unable to do such a thing. Adding a first step to St. Augustine's connundrum might help us to understand his reasoning.

1. not to be able not to sin;

2. to be able not to sin;

3. not to be able to sin.

Obviously number 2 is better than number 1 which is a tragic bondage. But number 2 is not the last word: it is not the final aim and hope of Christians and not to be compared with the joy of being, in a measure, free from the desire to sin.

We must be careful, however, not to interpret the freedom of "not able to sin" in an Apollinarian way, in which the powerlessness to sin is arrived at by destruction of the will. The truth is more like the movement from 2 to 3, in the case of a person's struggle with the temptation to waste time watching trivia on television and gradually finding oneself so untempted that one "cannot" spend one's time watching such banalities.

An interesting illustration of freedom that Nestorians fail to understand is provided in Nikos Kazantzakis's *The Last Temptation of Christ*. He presents a shocking scene—even more shocking by virtue that no logic of orthodoxy could prevent the reader from taking it seriously. In his novelist's imagination, Kazantzakis attempts to fill in something of Jesus' life before his public ministry. Mary Magdalene has known him from childhood and has understandably fallen deeply in love with him.

Jesus' sense of his own vocation precludes his responding in any manner that would entail marriage and family. With a love powerfully evoked but poignantly frustrated, she is driven to prostitution to find in quantity what was denied her in quality. Jesus himself understands a kind of complicity on his part, similar to that in Herod's slaughter of the innocents, which would not have occurred had he, the Christ, not been born. So he goes to assure her of his love, even though it is not the form of love she desires.

He must stand in line among her unwashed customers. When at last he enters her room, she is at first embarrassed and hurt by his very presence. But his exquisite love for her is expressed simply by his presence. He spends the night curled up on the floor of her room. Clearly he was not there for the same reason the others had come. He was not tempted, because his love for her had rendered him "not able to sin." It was not an Apollinarian powerlessness. As a man is a man, Jesus was a man. His profound love for her and the wisdom that it taught, that she needed him as a friend not as a customer, would not allow him to be tempted on a lesser level. Even sinful humans can sometimes experience movements from 2 to 3, as wisdom and deeper love render them not just "able not to sin" but give them a real measure of the truer freedom of "not being able to sin."

Kazantzakis was not permitted to be buried in holy ground. It is ironic that here, where he is the most shocking, he is most orthodox, and where he is least offensive, he is heretical. He describes Jesus levitating in mid air, not subject to the limits of time and space in much the same way as the primitive Docetics would have him be.

Sometimes people, reacting to the scandal (1 Cor. 1:23) of the incarnation and cross, readily accept the unbiblical picture of Christ refusing the limitations of his human condition. Kazantzakis did give us a picture in Christ of something like the freedom that is not forced or constrained but is a graceful flow from a sinless heart. This freedom is deeper and more desirable than an "ability not to sin" and is a refreshing contrast to the moralistic picture many have of the Christian life as one of control rather than freedom.

We have seen in this chapter the logical alliance of Pelagianism with Nestorianism that is the perennial soil of moralism. This alliance produced then, and produces today, some particularly cruel distortions of Christianity. They were characteristic of the school of Antioch from the earliest Adoptionists, through Paul of Samosata, and the soteriological aspects of Arianism, to Theodore of Mopsuestia and the Nestorians.

The view of freedom that is founded in scripture, resisted by sinful human nature, recovered by Augustine, followed by Bernard of Clairvaux (1090-1153), Thomas Aquinas (1225-74), Martin Luther (1483-1546), John Calvin (1509-64), and Thomas Cranmer (1489-1556), is an exotic idea in contemporary Western thought. The Adoptionist tradition, from Pelagians, Nestorians, Socinians, to Unitarians, continues to build its doctrine on an assumption of innate freedom that scripture promises as a gift and fruit. This assumption tends to determine their Christology, how they see the Christ.

Underlying the Nestorian two-person Christology, which falls short of true union necessary for salvation, is a common thread of confidence in the law and human ability to obey it and be saved. Contemporary Nestorians can be recognized by their inability to explain how Christ's "yoke is easy" *(Matt. 11:30)* when he has told them, "You, therefore, must be perfect, as your heavenly Father is perfect" *(Matt. 5:48)*. They are frequently unable to explain how the law is "holy, and just, and good" *(Rom. 7:12)* and at the same time the "strength of sin" *(1 Cor. 15:56)*. They find it difficult to accept that St. Paul teaches righteousness as the opposite of condemnation *(cf. 2 Cor. 3:9)*. The veil over their minds "remains unlifted" *(2 Cor. 3:14)* and the righteousness that declares itself in forgiveness of sins is not yet perceived.

The Council of Ephesus, by insisting on the unity of one person, condemned Nestorianism and rendered salvation accessible to sinners. In recognizing the human powerlessness to obey the absolute and just demands of the law, and the powerlessness of the law to save, the Council insisted on the union in one person of the two full natures of Christ and by that union saved salvation for sinners in the Christian gospel.

8

Eutychianism: The Religious Withering of Humanity

All heresies which touch the person of Jesus Christ, whether they have risen in these later days, or in any age heretofore, have occurred and do occur in terms of those heresies and those affirmations with which the Councils of Nicea, Constantinople, Ephesus, and Chalcedon dealt. In four words . . . truly, perfectly, indivisibly, distinctly: the first applied to His being God, and the second to His being Man, the third to His being of both One, and the fourth to His still continuing in that one Both: we may fully by way of abridgement comprise whatsoever antiquity hath at large handled either in declaration of Christian belief, or in refutation of the foresaid heresies.[1]

Richard Hooker

James Torrance tells an amusing story of his visit to the Holy Land. He had come back hot and dusty from a tour and was taking a shower in the men's dormitory. Another man, whom he did not know, was also showering. The stranger's opening remark was the question, "What do you think of Christ?" Torrance was a bit taken aback as it was not the kind of opening conversation he normally encountered in Edinburgh or Aberdeen. "I believe him to be the Son of the living God and Savior of the world." he replied. "Yes," came the response, "but how many natures?" "Two," answered Torrance, much to the obvious displeasure of his questioner; that ended the conversation.

Even in the twentieth century the issues of the fourth Ecumenical Council of Chalcedon in 451 stir passionate differences. The Council declared that there was in Christ, one person and two natures which has been the standard of orthodoxy for 1500 years in Roman Catholic, Eastern Orthodox, Anglican, Reformed, Lutheran, and Methodist churches.

This description of Christ satisfied neither all of the Nestorians nor all of the Monophysites. For centuries in Persia the Nestorians were the dominant Christian body, and they sent missionaries into both India and China. The Monophysites, on the other hand, still exist in great numbers as the Coptic Church in Egypt and a parallel church in Ethiopia, with others in Syria and Asia Minor, and a man in the shower in modern Jerusalem.

We have seen the pendulum swing from the Docetic and Alexandrian view of the Trinity as Sabellian to the Adoptionist and Antiochene opposite in Arianism (Nicaea 325). This in turn swung again to Apollinarianism (Constantinople 381) and back to Nestorianism (Ephesus 431). As could be guessed, a Docetic, Alexandrian type of heresy once again arose, but one somewhat more subtle than Apollinarianism.

The figure who gave his name to the last of the formal heresies we are treating was Eutyches (ca. 378 – ca. 452). He was an elderly, single-minded and unimaginative monk who responded negatively to the decisions of the Third General Council (Ephesus). He could not accept the Council's insistence on the two natures (*physis*), both human and divine in the unity of one person.

He was a close friend of Cyril of Alexandria and had been isolated most of his life from the Antiochene emphasis on the humanity of Christ. He had been strongly influenced by the

Alexandrian emphasis on spiritual unity with God, and this led him to become champion of the phrase "one incarnate nature (*physis*) of God the Word"—and this divine. Although he admitted a union of two natures before the incarnation, he would not accept that there were two natures after the incarnation.

He differed from Apollinarius in that the latter denied the full humanity at the outset, while Eutyches accepted a full humanity, but one that was absorbed into divinity in the very nature of the unity. Both men were termed Monophysites (one nature—*mono-physis*), and the same essential criticisms apply. Unlike Apollinarius, Eutyches appeared not to violate the axiom "What he did not assume, he could not redeem," but he clearly violated the other equally valuable axiom against all Docetic heresies, "Grace never destroys nature."

Remembering that whatever happens to Christ's humanity affects our salvation, we can see that Eutychianism is a "gospel" of destruction. The price of unity is Christ's (and our) humanity. This religious suicide is a characteristic temptation of all Docetic heresies. If Jesus' human nature is so absorbed in the union with the logos that it ceases to exist, then salvation means not the redemption of human nature but its loss and destruction. This heresy feeds upon and carries with it the human temptation to flee from flesh, body, and the claims of social justice. The portrait of Jesus without a full human nature is in stark contrast to the figure we meet in the gospels.

This contradiction of the simplest aspects of scripture cannot be explained with anything approaching cogency simply on the basis of theology, doctrine, and logic without including the insatiable human thirst for some way religion can help us escape our human condition in time and space. We are similarly tempted to escape when we see the historical mess surrounding the condemnation of Eutyches. He was first condemned for heresy by a synod under Flavian, Patriarch of Constantinople, but he had the powerful support of Dioscorus, Patriarch of Alexandria, who was motivated as much by jealousy of Constantinople and Rome as he was concerned with doctrine. Even more power-ful was his backing by Emperor Theodosius II, who considered that his best chance to unify the Empire was by encouraging the Monophysites.

Hence, the emperor, acting at the request of Dioscorus, called a council at Ephesus in 449. Flavian's synod was reversed and Eutyches vindicated. The Monophysites' theological disdain for the flesh was paralleled by their contempt for the flesh of Flavian, who was so roughly handled that he died as a result. The council was a stunning victory for the Patriarch of Alexandria and Eutyches. Pope Leo I of Rome had supported Flavian in a brief but brilliant statement (Leo's *Tome*) but his views were ignored and Leo himself was excommunicated by Dioscorus. Thus, the Patriarch of Alexandria had succeeded in removing Flavian, Patriarch of Constantinople, by death, removing Leo, the Pope of Rome, by excommunication, and repudiating what orthodoxy there was in the teachings at Antioch. Leo was under-standably upset and branded the council "a synod of robbers," as it has, thereafter, been called (*Latrocinium*).

In 450, Theodosius II fell off his horse and was killed. He was succeeded by his sister, Pulcheria, whose orthodox senti-ments were favorable to Leo. A council was called to meet at Chalcedon in 451.

This was the largest council ever assembled, with approxi-mately six hundred bishops present. Since Dioscorus was Cyril of Alexandria's nephew as well as his theological and patriarchal successor, his position was assured. Cyril's name carried the aura of orthodoxy with almost as much authority as that of Athanasius. Two expository letters written by Cyril against Nestorianism were part of the agenda. He had used the term "single nature" (*mia physis*), which seemed to help the position of Eutyches.

On the other hand, Leo's *Tome,* ignored by the "Synod of Robbers," was treated at Chalcedon with great respect, and it made a substantial contribution to the council. The council affirmed the creedal statement (Nicene Creed) of Nicaea and Constantinople. In opposition to the Nestorians, a new statement was added, which refuted the teaching of two persons in Christ and, in opposition to both the Apollinarians and Eutychians, insisted on two natures before and after union.

> Therefore, following the holy fathers, we all with one accord teach men to acknowledge one and the same Son, our Lord Jesus Christ, at once complete in Godhead and complete in manhood, truly God and truly man, consisting also of a reasonable soul and body; of one substance *(homoousios)* with the father as regards his Godhead, and at the same time of one substance with us as regards his manhood; like us in all respects, apart from sin; as regards his Godhead, begotten of the Father before the ages, but yet as regards his manhood begotten, for us men and for our salvation, of Mary the Virgin, the God-bearer *(Theotokos);* one and the same Christ, Son, Lord, Only-begotten, recognized in two natures, without confusion, without change, without division, without separation; the distinction of natures being in no way annulled by the union, but rather the characteristics of each nature being preserved and coming together to form one person and subsistence, not as parted or separated into two persons, but one and the same Son and Only-begotten God the Word, Lord Jesus Christ; even as the prophets from earliest times spoke of him and our Lord Jesus Christ himself taught us, and the creed of the Fathers has handed down to us.[2]

William Porcher DuBose gives the most adequate summary of this lasting contribution: "For the first time, along with the Athanasian statement of the real divinity of the incarnate Lord, there is posited something like a corresponding and adequate statement of the reality and actuality of his humanity."[3] The Council of Chalcedon came to be accepted as the Fourth General Council of the church and the authority on orthodoxy for virtually all of Christendom. It produced the "final" creed. Statements of faith since Chalcedon are called "confessions." It was no mean accomplishment. In spite of all the criticism it has received over the centuries, alternative "improvements" have gained little or no consensus.

From the time of its adjournment, critics accused this council of reverting to Nestorianism, with a triumph of the Antiochene school over the essential unity of the logos and human nature. On the other hand, some in recent times claim that it was essentially Monophysite in its approval of Cyril's letters and denial of a particular, individual human personality of Jesus. It did not, however, appear to be Nestorian to the contemporary Nestorians nor Monophysite to the contemporary Monophysites, down to today's man in the shower in Jerusalem.

The validity of continuing questions about Chalcedon lies in the fact that the council, admittedly, did not explain how there can be a unity in Christ without losing either of his natures. It only asserted this fact. It did not so much explain, as set limits. However, so-called "improvements" on Chalcedon, tried through the centuries and into the present time, appear to be merely new versions of Docetism or Adoptionism. As long as human nature continues to be tempted toward escape or self-centeredness, these two challenges to the limits set by the church at Chalcedon will appeal to theologians as well as to popular minds.

One aspect of Chalcedonian orthodoxy is especially offensive to modern ears: the insistence that the humanity of Christ—Incarnation—is an "impersonal humanity." To some this seems to mean the absence in Christ of a distinctive human person. The formula: one divine person in two natures renders Christ, it is claimed, to be less than fully human because he lacked a human personality.

The word "impersonal" has a pejorative ring to it in modern ears, with its connotation of something less than human. Yet the Council meant no such thing. In fact, when, at one point, the council was satisfied with the phrase "*of* two natures," the imperial commissioners expressed disapproval, pointing out to the bishops that Dioscorus and Eutyches could accept "*of* two natures," in the sense that Christ's unity was made *out of* two natures but so "spiritualized" that the human nature no longer existed.

The council agreed and changed the phrase to the crucial *"in two natures"* showing the clear intention of preserving the lasting integrity of Christ's human nature. This does not, however, resolve the problem of the "impersonal" humanity asserted at Chalcedon. Certainly if it meant something less than human by "impersonal," it is indeed a new version of Apollinarianism or Eutychianism with their respective "one nature" (mono-physis-ism) teaching.

The problem underlying this dilemma is a philosophical one and many people in the twentieth century find it difficult to believe that philosophy can have any relevance to anything important. This attitude is fatal to any appreciation of realities underlying appearances and to any firm grasp on the guidelines given by Chalcedon. As we have noted, it has been said with some truth that "every person is essentially a Platonist or an Aristotelian." A popular philosophy of the Hellenistic world of the fifth century was a form of Platonism (Neoplatonism), whereas, today, the overwhelming popular world-view is Aristotelian.

The fathers at the Council of Chalcedon were assuming that what made all tables tables was the universal idea of table, the *form* or *reality* of which made tables what they are and not something else. Similarly when they thought of "humanity," they thought of that reality or essence ("substance") that gave rise to all humanity and made humans humans and not squirrels or donkeys.

Thus, this council, insisting that the one divine person (*hypostasis*) of Jesus included both a divine and a human nature, thereby established the fact that the humanity saved by God's action in the incarnation includes all that is human, both Gentiles and women, not merely an individual male Jew named Jesus in the first century. Remembering the Cappodocian axiom that "what he did not assume, he could not save," we know that the humanity indwelt by the divine logos must be that which gives rise to and is the reality of all humans. As early as New Testament times the full inclusion of Gentiles and women was resisted by some. Christ's inclusive humanity is necessary for any to be saved and cannot be relegated to the individual Jesus alone.

St. Paul established the guidelines for all subsequent orthodoxy that race, nationality, degree of servitude, and gender are not barriers to identification with Christ's saving humanity, and it is an Antiochene heresy to say that any of these differences is a barrier. This inclusive humanity is what the Council was striving to safeguard by its use of the term "impersonal" humanity. To be faithful to the fifth century meaning, perhaps the word "impersonal" is better translated for our modern ears as "inclusive" humanity, in much the same way as "substance" is better understood as "essence" in today's materialistic climate.

It still must be conceded that the Council of Chalcedon set limits rather than fully explained how there could be one Christ while preserving both natures. Contemporary critics, such as Anthony Hanson and Norman Pittenger, raise questions regarding the adequacy of Chalcedon's teaching that there is one person (divine) and two natures (divine and human). While properly raising the question of its residual Monophysitism, these critics must themselves face the alternatives lest we begin again to teach "one faith, one baptism" and two Lords (persons), as in Nestorianism.[4]

Gerald Bray explains that in Jesus'

> human nature the divine person lived a normal human life, not abandoning the attributes of his divine nature, but not allowing them to distort the human nature by removing its limitations. Put in the most simple language, Jesus could be fully God without knowing, as a man, the secrets of nuclear physics or even how to use a telephone. His omniscience as God did not automatically carry over into his life on earth as a man.[5]

The foundation for this understanding Bray finds in the thought of two men both named Leontius, one of Byzantium, the other of Jerusalem, and in the teaching of Chalcedon by the church, expecially in the East after 451.

Coming from a culture generally characterized by naturalistic and materialistic forms more akin to Aristotelian philosophy (rationalism, nominalism, and individualism) than to the Neoplatonic thought of Chalcedon, it is not surprising that modern critics tend to object to Chalcedon's alleged Monophysitism. In contrast, earlier critics of Chalcedon accused the council of capitulating to the Nestorian and Antiochene side by accepting Leo's *Tome.*

Unfortunately, Eutychianism, like the other heresies, was not altogether dispelled by the council but continues to appear throughout history, being particularly insidious as it frequently wears the garments of orthodoxy. Eutychianism fits the popular idea that orthodoxy is "spiritual" and is always ready to emerge as the winds of flight and escape blow across the human heart.

The tradition of mysticism is especially susceptible to the Eutychian escape. Perhaps nowhere is Eutychianism better formulated than by Meister Eckhardt: "Thou must be pure in heart, and only that heart is pure which has exterminated creaturehood."[6] The clear Christian hope expressed in *1 Cor.* 15:38 ("But God gives it a body as he has chosen, and to each kind of seed its own body") is not that human uniqueness is lost, or destroyed, in the promise of eternal life, but that it is changed and fulfilled. "Grace never destroys nature" is a constant guard against all types of Docetic heresies. Unfortunately, many "orthodox," who are weary of doing battle against Nestorianism in its contemporary forms of Socinianism and Unitarianism, go "on retreat" and absorb uncritically devotional writings that err in the opposite direction. Evelyn Underhill is widely regarded as one of the greatest spiritual writers of the twentieth century. Nonetheless, even she fails to escape the endemic weakness of mysticism.

She defines worship as "the response of the creature to the Eternal" and as "the acknowledgement of the Transcendent."

She claims that worship "always means God and the priority of God."[7] If this were true we would never need the second commandment. Our Old Testament experience illustrates again and again the overwhelming temptation to worship anything other than the living God. Worship is too frequently not the "acknowledgement of the Transcendent," and it does not invariably "mean God and the priority of God."

We worship fertility cults, money, celebrities, heroines, heroes, and bellies ("whose God is their belly, and whose glory is their shame, who mind earthly things"—*Phil. 3:19AV*) and like Eutychians we escape from our human condition into a spiritual realm where our humanity and individuality are lost as a drop in "the ocean of God."

These escapes in some extreme forms of mysticism, uncritically nurtured in the very bosom of what appears to be orthodox, are recurring manifestations of Eutychianism—a promise of the withering away of the human individuality by the very process of one's "salvation." This mystical loss *of* self rather than death *to* self in baptism is what led Reinhold Niebuhr to call mysticism the "suicide of the ego" and Dean Inge of St. Paul's Cathedral to say that mysticism "begins in mist, is centered in I, and ends in schism."

In fairness it must be said that these criticisms are not applicable to all mysticism, especially that of St. Bernard of Clairvaux, whose robust, active political life and sensitive pastoral wisdom show no Eutychian flight but a courageous willingness to risk his "spirit in substantiation." However, the many unfortunate mystical and devotional works that deserve this criticism indicate again the wisdom of Jeremy Taylor and Samuel Taylor Coleridge that "heresy is not an error of the understanding but an error of the will."

People who are drawn into these new forms of Eutychianism are often those who are clearly and enthusiastically committed to the creeds. They are frequently forthright in their objection to the heresies that stem from the Antiochene side. Critics of

Bishop James Pike correctly saw the Adoptionist direction his teachings on the Trinity were taking, but they were often blind to the Eutychian drift of many mystical writings. The value of these Chalcedonian limits is that they cut both ways and are as needful and useful today as they were in the fifth century.

The mysterious and paradoxical nature of both the Trinity and Christology should not be dispelled. The council's conclusions are not explanations of the mystery of God's being but perimeters saving us from distortions of God's revelation. The barriers that keep us from the awesome wonder of true worship are more frequently in our minds or hearts than in the doctrinal limits that guide us as we approach such mystery.

Perhaps an analogy would help us understand why it is impossible to have a unity of divine and human natures without losing one or the other, or without denying the unity by a final assertion of two persons. Most of us would assume that a gallon of water mixed with a gallon of alcohol would fill a two-gallon container. But, because of the molecular structure of water and alcohol, there is a blend in which some of the spaces between the molecules of each are occupied by the other. The space necessary to contain a gallon of each is thereby reduced. A gallon of water plus a gallon of alcohol do not together fill a two-gallon container.

If we remember that human nature was made "in the image of God" and that Christ did not assume sinful, fallen nature but true, sinless humanity, then such a blend of his humanity and his divinity can be seen as one person without the loss of either.

This simple analogy of water and alcohol is helpful as long as we remember that in such a blend neither the essence of water nor the essence of alcohol is lost, as the essence of Christ's divinity and his humanity are not lost in some mixture but fit together. Water and alcohol blend but are not completely congruent, and therefore together they represent something more than each but less than the sum of both. Unlike water and alcohol, the perfect humanity assumed at the incarnation is that original and sinless humanity made in the image of God. The original image of humans, lost through Adam's disobedience, and now restored in Christ's obedience, discloses the divinity that we shall at the end have in Christ *(1 John 3:2).* Thus, what we see in the divinity and humanity of Christ is not a partial blend, as in water and alcohol, but a complete and perfect congruity in which neither divinity nor humanity is lost in the unity of one person with a divine personality. This very congruity, of true and all-inclusive sinless humanity with God is the wondrous result of the "torn veil" between God and us. The righteousness of God is no longer the source of terror and condemnation *(2 Cor. 3:9, John 3:17, Rom. 8:1,34).* The justice of God has not been lowered or compromised. The human tendency toward self-centeredness that inhibits and hides human glory is not winked at or denied but given access to redemption in Christ.

Like the other heresies, Eutychianism continues to contaminate the faith of contemporaries. The teaching, that after the incarnation the human nature of Christ withers away or is absorbed into his divinity, leads people to believe that our being spiritual like Christ means that our human nature and its limitations are overcome. On the contrary, Christ himself is depicted in scripture as having the kind of human nature that grows weary, hungers, thirsts, is hurt by scourging, thorns, nails and the spear, and dies.

The attraction of Eutychian teaching, however, is ever present, and many believe that "truly spiritual" persons will not be subject to sickness, but, if they are, they will invariably be healed because of their exceptional spirituality. The Rev. David Watson, one of the recent outstanding leaders in the Church of England, developed cancer and died. Many of his followers believed that he was "too spiritual" to have cancer, but that if he did indeed have cancer he would surely be healed. His courageous book, *Fear No Evil,* written during his illness shortly before his death, is an orthodox corrective to the Eutychianism that cruelly renders us unprepared for the abiding humanness and inevitable suffering that is Christ's and ours in this life.

Chalcedon's claim, that a fully divine nature and an undiminished human nature are united in the one Christ, assures Christians that grace does not destroy nature in its redemption. Chalcedon maintains the vision of Athanasius, "he became as we are in order that we may become as he is," and the vision promised in *1 John 3:2:* "Beloved, we are God's children now, it does not yet appear what we shall be, but we know that when he appears we shall be like him, for we shall see him as he is."

The historic attacks on Chalcedon from the Alexandrian and Docetic side (Monophysites) plus the contemporary criticism from the Antiochian and Adoptionist side (Nestorianism) should not be allowed to obscure the gracious miracle of this council as expressed by Douglas John Hall.

> Given the enormous pressure under which faith in that age of the human race must certainly have found itself—namely the pressure to come up with another god—the Formula of Chalcedon is itself nothing short of a miracle.[8]

9

A Rectitude of the Heart

"We strain to glimpse your mercy seat
And find you kneeling at our feet."

These lines from Brian Wrenn's hymn evoke the
sort of conceptual revision that is needed if we take
seriously the Trinity, not as a formula from the past,
but as a requirement to go again to the roots of
our understanding of God.[1]

Colin Gunton

We saw that it took two councils to set the limits of orthodoxy against the Adoptionist influence of Antioch and two Councils to set the limits against the Docetic influence of Alexandria. Newcomers to early church history are frequently shocked to see the political and sinful context in which the empire and the church hammered out these teaching guidelines.

The empire frequently used the church to justify its order. The intrigues of court and political rivalries often affected theological deliberations. Church leaders themselves were not immune to jealousies and party strife. The rivalries among the great patriarchal cities frequently influenced the doctrinal debates. These contaminating factors were constantly present as the profound doctrinal guidelines were developed, drawing out the inevitable implications of knowing Jesus Christ as Lord without violating the radical monotheism of the first commandment.

Reflecting on this historical experience, Christians can be reassured when faced with the inevitable ambiguities and sin in each age. This realization is a good corrective to our seeing the period of the early church as some golden age of the past to which we are tempted to return. It can dissipate the self-pity and despair that arise in the frustrations and ambiguities of any subsequent age, including our own.

Another surprise to most readers is the precariousness of orthodoxy and how unusual it was for any teaching to be a balanced formulation, uncontaminated by excesses from one direction or another. These conciliar contributions to Christian orthodoxy were the result, not of deliberations by a broad base of Christians believing and understanding the views of Irenaeus, Athanasius, and the Cappadocians, but of agreement by many who were relieved to accept the definition of the councils to avoid what they considered even greater deviations. The guidelines were, in fact, only established with the aid of heretics because there were never enough orthodox leaders sufficiently untainted by either of the two tendencies to have established the limits themselves. It took some Arians to help defeat the Sabellians in 269, some Apollinarians (e.g. Apollinarius himself) to defeat the Arians in 325 (Nicaea), some Nestorians (e.g. Theodore of Mopsuestia) to help against the Apollinarians in 381 (Constantinople), and some Eutychians to draw the limits against Nestorianism in 431. There was not a sufficiently broad base left in 451 (Chalcedon) to prevent a lasting schism by the limits set at this council. For example, the Coptic Monophysite church still exists in Egypt and Ethiopia.

If the numerical base for orthodoxy was astonishingly small, the religious and theological playing area marked off by these councils is remarkably broad. The length of the orthodox field is marked by the line asserting God's personal agency in our salvation (against the Arian outside boundaries), the line claiming that human nature is not destroyed in redemption (against the Apollinarian outside boundaries), the line claiming the unity of Christ in one person (against the Nestorian two-person Jesus), and the line that assures us that our humanity is fulfilled and not to be withered away (against Eutychianism).

In spite of popular notions to the contrary, it is heresy, not orthodoxy, that is narrow. G.K. Chesterton's observation is accurate: "Every heresy has been an attempt to narrow the church."[2] Orthodoxy's unfortunate reputation is caused in part by the same dynamic we have seen in the development of various heresies that pander to our fallen wills. Like a child who believes his parents are "narrow" because they will not give him a gross of chocolate bars, so the orthodox boundaries against making Christianity a flight from life or a blessing on our self-centeredness are resented by the spiritually immature as "narrow."

Gresham's Law in economics states that bad currency tends to drive good currency out of circulation. A similar law in religion adds an additional factor: the false image of orthodoxy. When one speaks of Jesus as though one had just finished lunch with him, many will forebear using his name at all. When believers speak as though they see, not as St. Paul "through a glass darkly," but even now as "face to face," many listeners become skeptical in the face of such exaggerated certainties. When the religious and biblical "language of Sion" is used in frivolous sentimentality or to legitimize aggression, or to disguise an otherwise naked greed for money or power; then authentic use of the language of Christian faith tends to be hoarded and driven out of circulation and we are left with such pale euphemisms as a "Higher Power" or "The Force."

Traditional Christianity has a special obligation to reflect an authentic orthodoxy lest it continue to "debase the coinage" in heretical use of the language of Sion. The contemporary scene is perceived by the media to be divided between conservative and liberal theologians. As superficial as this division is in both politics and in theology, there is some truth to it.

Liberal theologians have tended, until recently, to be doing the Adoptionist thing all over again, and, in some cases, without even admitting a delegated divinity for Jesus. They have been marked by a candor in print and pulpit concerning what they do not believe, a candor not matched by their actions, which would mean leaving their avowedly Trinitarian denominations and becoming honest Unitarians.

At the same time this has left conservative churchmen appearing to occupy the historically high but culturally disdained ground of orthodoxy. The learned theologian Harold O.J. Brown, himself a conservative Protestant, warns us of this facile assumption.

> No one since the fourth century has called himself an Apollinarian, but the idea of Apollinaris resurfaces wherever there is a combination of orthodox dogmatism and theological naivete. Much modern twentieth century conservative Protestantism is implicitly Apollinarian because, while it ringingly confesses the deity of Christ, it finds it hard to think that he was really a man.[3]

In *American Piety,* a book published in 1968, two sociologists, Charles Glock and Rodney Stark, defined orthodoxy as "belief in God, divinity of Christ, and in life after death." Their sociological studies show that the culture is moving away from these beliefs and, if the church is to survive, it must relinquish and give up these beliefs.

Customer research showed Studebaker that people were not buying Studebaker cars and the survival of the company depended on their getting into some other line of work. Similarly, since the cultural customers were increasingly unwilling to buy orthodoxy, as the research of Glock and Stark showed the decline in numbers of the so-called "brand name" denominations, the church to survive must get into some other line of work. (They actually violated their own research that showed that Pentecostal and fundamentalist churches were growing. The authors' commercial slant should have urged the "main line" churches to become Pentecostal and fundamentalist.) The remarkable significance of Glock and Stark's book is that its definition of orthodoxy would embrace all the Docetic heresies and almost all the Adoptionist heresies. Christian orthodoxy is a strange and wondrous thing, unknown to many scholars and to many conventional Christians.

What these sociologists did reflect, however, is the overwhelming drift in Western culture since the seventeenth century in the direction of what is most congenial to the preoccupations of Antiochene Christianity. The confidence in reason helped to dispel the lingering magic and superstition and, in the eighteenth and nineteenth centuries, led to the unprecedented achievements of science and industry. All aspects of Docetism seem to belong to a long ago and unregretted past. Divine beings, spiritual realities, and a creation suspected as the source of evil, if not evil itself, seemed no longer imaginable to the mind of modern humanity fixed upon the apparently unlimited human accomplishments of jets, penicillin, satellites, computers, and monofilament fishing line.

Of course, some in the Romantic Movement were disillusioned by the horrifying abuses perpetrated by the French Revolution in the name of reason. And, on a personal level, there were always individuals who expressed doubts about the culture's sufficiency to resolve the problems of being human. The timeless dilemma of the "one and the many" remained unresolved and, beneath the surface of cultural optimism, haunting and unsettling rumblings were expressed, most frequently by poets and playwrights.

Matthew Arnold's "Dover Beach" ("ignorant armies clash by night"), W. B. Yeats' "The Second Coming" ("and what rough beast, its hour come round at last, slouches toward Bethlehem to be born?"), and T.S. Eliot's "The Rock" ("men have forgotten /all gods except Usury, Lust and Power") are examples of poets who saw beneath the surface of cultural confidence. The plays of Henrik Ibsen, Eugene O'Neill, and Tennessee Williams disclosed an agony of the heart that belied the facile optimism of their times.

Yet the broad stream of Western thought since the seventeenth century has been characterized by a confidence more congenial to Pelagianism than at any time in history. And Pelagianism is the banana peel on the cliff of Unitarianism. Harvard College, founded by the most orthodox of trinitarian Puritans, was not seventy years old when Yale was founded explicitly to correct the unitarianism of Harvard. As a denomination, Unitarianism has never flourished numerically, but the teaching has eaten its way into the heart of the trinitarian traditions.

The rise of Socinianism (mentioned in chapter 2), a modern version of Adoptionism, with its special influence in universities and in Protestantism, has accelerated the drift toward unitarianism. The Socinians taught that Jesus was a good man. He obeyed the law, was adopted as the Son of God, is now a hearer of prayer, and was granted a delegated divinity as a reward, that we will share when we have done as Jesus did.

Textbooks on doctrine inadvertently mislead us when they put "unitarianism" under the category of doctrines about God and the Trinity Although this is academically correct, the human factor so frequently overlooked is that unitarianism does not begin with someone scratching his head about three in one or one in three. Historically, it began not with the doctrine of God but with the doctrine of human nature.

When human nature is regarded as sufficient to fulfill God's law by its will power, all one needs is to be given the law and the example of Jesus and exhorted to obey and follow. The Trinity becomes irrelevant. This approach squeezes out of the doctrine of the Atonement all substance but the exemplary theme which becomes a law we must follow: be like Jesus. This leads inevitably to an Adoptionist Christology and to a unitarian deity.

Samuel Taylor Coleridge, although a son of an Anglican clergyman, absorbed early in life the assumptions of this cultural drift and became committed to unitarianism. His personal experience of the bankruptcy of Pelagianism, however, led to his deeper conversion and to a firm grasp of how misleading is this first "slip" in Christian doctrine. Recognizing the Pelagianism in the popular seventeenth century bishop Jeremy Taylor, Coleridge summed up three hundred years of cultural drift in one sentence: "In short, Socinianism (Pelagianism and Adoptionism) is as inevitable a deduction from Taylor's scheme as Deism or Atheism is from Socinianism."[4]

Conservative theologians have too frequently attempted to stop this drift along the line of Christology and the Trinity without proper attention to how these teachings apply to us sinners. An accurate understanding of human nature and the way that God's gracious action in Christ has given us a new relationship with him discloses these dogmas of Trinity and Christology as indispensable good news. If left hanging in academic air, unrelated to our human condition, they become burdens to be imposed or needless baggage to be left behind.

Adolf von Harnack has taught us as much about the history of the church as almost anyone, and yet he himself held Adoptionist views of Christ, defending the second- and third-century Adoptionist teachers as the true critical thinkers of their day. He admits that their cold rationalism could not have inspired the courage of martyrdom and would doubtless not have survived the persecutions.[5]

Harnack's Adoptionism is indicated also in his denigration of the death and resurrection of Christ. He believed the fundamental principal of Christianity to be "the Fatherhood of God and the brotherhood of man," not the death and resurrection of Christ. Here, the human factor is apparent. His is not merely an error of intellect but an error of ingratitude. The only way we can call God "Father," is as gift, by the death and resurrection of Christ. Neither Moses nor Elijah, but only Christ enabled us to have such a relationship.

What has been procured for us as a gift and at great cost,

Harnack now arrogates to the very nature of things. He disdains the teaching that the cross and Easter are essential, emptying them of their costly role in making us children by adoption *(Rom. 8:15 and Gal. 4:5)* and grace. Instead he arrogates to humans the entitlement and "right" to call God "Father." He insists that this privilege is the innate condition of all humans, independent of what God has done in Christ.

In today's popular view of religion, we are more the victims of Harnack's accommodation to the spirit of his age than we are recipients of the good news of scripture. The word "Father" for God occurs only eleven times in the Old Testament, and not as God's name but as a title. George Washington was given the title "Father of his Country" but that was not his name. In the New Testament the term "Father" occurs 261 times and it is God's name. In Thomas Cranmer's Service of Holy Communion we say "And now, as our Savior Christ has taught us, *we are bold to say* [italics mine], Our Father. . . ."

That which Abraham, Moses, and Elijah were not privileged to say, we, because of our adoption as children of God through the only begotten Son, now are able to say "our Father." It is characteristic of human arrogance to take what is given as gift and make of it a right, an entitlement. The fruit of the Spirit, joy, cannot exist without gratitude. When gifts are reduced to rights, gratitude and its flower, joy, disappear. Humans are notorious for taking the gifts of ethnic origin, money, and talents and converting them into rights and pedestals of superiority.

Harnack has led the way down this cul de sac of reducing our gift of privilege in saying "our Father" to a universal, in-born, innate right. Harnack claimed that the fundamental principle of Christianity is the "Fatherhood of God and the brotherhood of man." He took the "Fatherhood" that was given by the crucifixion and resurrection of Christ and claimed it as an innate human right.

Harnack's error is certainly not simply an academic matter of research and scholarship. Theologians, even the greatest of them, can be greatly wrong, because wrong about gospel is not so much a wrong of the mind as a wrong of the heart. Ingratitude is among the most ubiquitous and tenacious of sins, which neither intelligence nor scholarship invariably prevents.

The Council of Ephesus made a significant contribution to guidelines against Adoptionism with its condemnation of the Pelagian view, that salvation depends on the power of human will to overcome sin. But infinitely more effective against the pervasive Adoptionism that arises spontaneously from the fallen human heart, as well as from the see of Antioch, are the birth narratives in Matthew and Luke. The confidence that Jesus was the unusually good man who was "adopted" as a deity and became merely an example for us to follow is radically undercut by the message of the angel.

The tragic story of human patterns of reducing gifts into pretensions is not only true of inherited wealth and being "well-born," but also of spiritual gifts. "Being chosen" is, at the outset, the humblest doctrine in Scripture, yet the "idol factory" of the human heart most readily elevates such a gift to the highest pedestal of superiority. Combining this religious pretension with the genealogical one ("we are children of Abraham" through whom the Messiah will come) resulted in an arrogance unfit to be a manger for the humble Lord—unfit until humbled by the fact that the long, seemingly irrelevant genealogy of Joseph is brought to an abrupt stop: "and Mary is great with child by the Holy Spirit."

The story of Jesus' birth brings religious arrogance, masculine pride, and genetic pretense to naught after the lengthy genealogy ends with discontinuity and the intervention of God, bringing to naught the human pride of Joseph's ancestry. Doubts about the Virgin Birth almost always occur from Adoptionists. Their unwillingness to accept the stories is likely to be not so much a reluctance of the mind as a reluctance of the heart.

Adoptionism is not as strong a current at the end of the twentieth century as it was at its beginning. Many factors in recent history have made the teachings of Alexandria, with their characteristic heresies, more congenial to modern people. Modern science does not give the support to materialism and rationalism that it seemed to give in Newtonian physics. World wars, the bomb, the perceived failure of culture to civilize or civilization to redeem, have given many an appreciation once again of teachings associated with Alexandria—its values but also its Docetic and heretical tendencies.

Dr. Elisabeth Kübler-Ross is a good example of this recent shift from Antiochene to Alexandrian thought in our own age. Perhaps no single person has accomplished as much in leading a whole culture, not just doctors and nurses, to the long-neglected concern for the dying. The Antiochene culture that had drifted into almost complete secularism (the view that "this world is all there is") understandably was embarrassed by the fact of death. The very subject of death became as taboo to the twentieth century as sex seemed to be to the Victorians.

Studies showed how the dying have been inadvertently treated as pariahs, left alone and neglected by a culture embarrassed, in its self-assurance and Promethean confidence, by its failure to fix death. Dr. Kübler-Ross became the personification of kindness and attention to the terminally ill, the inspiration for countless hospices. Her studies on death and dying have been helpful and comforting to those hurt and bewildered by watching a loved one going through the irrational stages often involved in the process of dying.

The Alexandrian confidence, that this world is not the only or the last reality makes death more easily faced. The conviction that the human predicament is finally too great for anything but divine initiative and divine agency saves the Alexandrians from the Antiochene presumptions that lead inevitably to despair.

But along with the advantages come the Docetic temptations. Dr. Kübler-Ross' courage in the face of mortality brought with it a Platonic belief in the innate immortality of the soul. Death is no great tragedy for the individual, because all that is lost is a body. The soul, for Plato, is innately eternal and immortal. Death cannot touch it.

For the Christian, death is real and there is a radical discontinuity between Good Friday and Easter. The difference between Socrates' drinking hemlock and Jesus' agony in the garden of Gethsemane is the difference between confidence in one's own innate necessary immortality and one's utter dependence upon God to overcome the discontinuity of death in the reality of resurrection.

Neoplatonism, so much a part of the Alexandrian scheme, often carries with it the cultic worship of unseen spirits and entities that are a part of the Docetic temptations. Unfortunately, Elizabeth Kübler-Ross was involved in a cult in which she was introduced to her own personal entity, "Salem," and which celebrated bizarre fertility rites. Such occurences are characteristic of Gnosticism even in the twentieth century.[7]

Astrology, witches' covens, and new and strange cults seem to be thriving as we have not seen since the seventeenth century. The Christian church today must be prepared to meet not only the well-known adversary in the Adoptionist tendencies in and outside its membership, but a newly flourishing and even more dangerous distortion in the Docetic direction.

The exhortation to relinquish the very term "heresy" except as it applies to the early church, as was recommended in the book *Theological Freedom and Social Responsibilities*[8] and advocated more recently by Professor John Macquarrie,[9] would leave us defenseless against the contemporary cruelties of distorted teaching. This recommendation does, however, show how urgently needed it is for orthodoxy to be seen as good news defending us from bad news. A new vision of orthodoxy is indicated by Coleridge's description of faith as the "rectitude of the heart." The history and theology of the Christian faith must include the human factor. As we hear and retell the gospel, we unwittingly distort the story, thus reinforcing any heresy of which we may be a victim.

Inasmuch as our heart yet desires to flee life itself, the Gnostic and Docetic heresies will find fertile ground in which to grow. Inasmuch as our heart is yet self-centered and resists the implication of Christian baptism to die to self and be centered in Christ, Antiochene and Adoptionist heresies will be far more appealing than the scriptural story. Orthodoxy, then, will depend ultimately on our heart's desire to risk "spirit in substantiation," to follow in life the implications of the incarnation. At the same time, only a heart centered in The Center will find itself lost in "wonder, love and praise."

A heart without rectitude will betray orthodoxy by tone and spirit even if it is correct teaching. The heart's temptation to escape the ambiguities and problems of life and to establish its own self as center always contributes to any distortion of the gospel. The heart itself must bow in continual worship before God, whose name is Father, Son and Holy Spirit, to be saved from its escape into death and from its prison of self-centeredness.

10

Orthodoxy and Pagan Religions Revived

The New Age has reopened a door closed since Christianity drove out the demons from the woods, desacralized the natural world and generally took a dim view of excessive interest in the affairs of Satan's kingdom of fallen angels. Now they are back, knocking on university dorm doors, sneaking around psychology laboratories and chilling the spines of ouija players. Modern folk have fled from grandfather's clockwork universe to great-great grandfather's chamber of gothic horrors![1]

James W. Sire

For the time is coming when people will not endure sound teaching, but having itching ears they will accumulate for themselves teachers to suit their own likings, and will turn away from listening to the truth and wander into myths.

2 Tim. 4:3-4

Struggling with heresies is something of a luxury compared with dealing with the rebirth of ancient religions and new cults in modern society. The so-called "New Age" movement, although a loosely organized one, is having a pervasive influence upon our times, with its ideas seeping into our culture through television, movies, science fiction, school and college curriculums, courses for business executives, schools of therapy and our churches. In spite of its wide diversity, three basic teachings seem to be generally characteristic of the movement.

First, all is one. In spite of appearances to the contrary there are no real distinctions between God and human beings, between persons and things, between you and me, or even between good and evil. All are expressions of the same single reality. That the individual self or soul is at the same time the universal self or soul is a belief found in Hinduism. As a philosophy it is called monism.

Secondly, all is God. This is the same pantheism that we have seen the early church confront in Gnosticism. A leading contemporary spokesperson for the movement is the moviestar Shirley MacLaine. She insists that everyone is a god, although we may be ignorant of it. When we do realize that we are gods, the world will be a happier and healthier place than it is now. She also claims that each of us has lived before in a previous existence and will live again. There is no death, only a passing to another reincarnation. We are the agents of our own realities, because we as gods create them.[2] She is by no means the only representative of these views, but her books have sold millions of copies and her ideas are widely disseminated on talk shows and in expensive, but well attended, lectures.

Thirdly, all is well. A profound optimism is characteristic of New Agers. They see themselves standing on the very threshold of the millennium. Because all is one, and all is God, we humans are gods and we have unlimited potential for personal transformation. They share a belief in the innate goodness and trustworthiness of humans with the popular psychology of Abraham Maslow and Carl Rogers of the so-called Human Potential Movement.[3] Like the Gnosticism of old, humans are saved not by repentance and forgiveness, but by knowledge.

We don't need to repent; we only need to know, and when we do, all will be well. This transformation by knowledge has nothing to do with morality.

Lesslie Newbigin comments:

> The New Age movement, for all the validity of its protest and the value of some of its recommendations, is in truth a very old blind alley. There is a very long history to remind us of what happens when nature is our ultimate point of reference, from the Ba'al worshippers of the Old Testament to the worshippers of blood and soil in Nazi Germany. Nature knows no ethics. There is no right and wrong in nature; the controlling realities are power and fertility. Nature sometimes has a charming smile, but her teeth are terrible.[4]

These ideas, like the heresies we have studied, readily appeal to the worst aspect of our nature. "Ye shall be as gods" is as flattering now as it has been since the Garden of Eden. "All is one," "all is God," and "all is well" is as attractive to adults as dessert before dinner is to a child. Would the realities of the Balkans, inner-city blight, troubled marriages, rebellious children, and irresponsible parents be any less difficult to solve if we all believed we were gods? On the contrary, humans trying to be gods is precisely what is wrong in the Balkans, our cities, our marriages, our children, our parents, and in ourselves.

G.K. Chesterton saw the danger in this sort of religion when he claimed that

> Of all horrible religions the most horrible is the worship of the god within. Anyone who knows anybody knows how it would work; . . . that Jones shall worship the god within turns out ultimately to mean that Jones shall worship Jones. Let Jones worship the sun or moon, anything rather than the Inner-Light; let Jones worship cats or crocodiles, if he can find any in his street, but not the god within.[5]

Other versions of "we are gods" can be seen in some schools of psychology. The teachings of Carl Gustaf Jung not only took cognizance of religion and regarded it as essential to psychological health, but, at the same time, he encouraged the belief that the self is God. "God is our own longing to which we pay divine honours."[6] Like aspects of the New Age movement, Jungian psychology has affinities with Hindu and Buddhist ideas.

After decades of anti-religious polemic from Freudians, it was at first refreshing to welcome the writings of Scott Peck who, like Jung, took religion quite seriously. Few authors have been more widely read in the last two decades than Peck. However, when he wrote *The Road Less Traveled,* he had not been baptized, and he joined in the contemporary siren chorus telling us that we are gods.

> In my vision the collective unconscious is God. [Mental illness occurs] when the conscious will of the individual deviates substantially from the will of God, which is the individual's own unconscious will. . . . Since the unconscious is God all along, we may further define the goal of spiritual growth to be the attainment of godhead by the conscious self. It is for the individual to become totally, wholly God."[7]

Behind the affirmation that humans are gods is the monist assertion that all is one. This is not a benign teaching. The Oxford scholar R.C. Zaehner, a leading authority on mysticism, has shown the influence of this now popular religion on Charles Manson. Monism denies the distinctions between God and creation, God and us, good and evil. Zaehner insists that when Manson orchestrated and ordered the ritual murder of actress Sharon Tate, he was absolutely sane. He had been to the place promised by monism where there is neither good nor evil.

Douglas Groothius quotes Zaehner's insistence that Manson's atrocities

> were not insane but logical, given Manson's monistic viewpoint. Because he believed in the One, "many a 'rich pig' was to meet a gruesome and untimely end . . . Charlie, so far from being mad had a lucidly logical mind . . ." According to an acquaintance,

Manson "believed you could do no wrong, no bad. Everything was good. Whatever you do, you are following your own Karma."[8]

One can see why Chesterton believed this sort of religion to be "the most horrible" of all. Most Christians, like the proverbial French generals who keep fighting the *last* war, are not prepared after three hundred years of fighting the Antiochene/Adoptionist drift of the Enlightenment—rationalism, unitarianism, reductionism, and atheism—to engage the present enemy, which comes from the more ancient Alexandrian/ Gnostic direction.

When people believe in God, and genuinely claim to be religious, it does not necessarily mean they are Christian. The early church knew its greatest enemies were not the Stoic atheists but the very religious Gnostics and pantheists who either repudiated Christianity entirely or attempted to absorb it by twisting it in Docetic directions.

What is particularly alarming is the casualness with which these and similar teachings are being received into the churches. Such contemporary theologians as Sallie McFague of Vanderbilt, Grace Jantzen of England, and the Roman Catholic Matthew Fox embrace a monism that objects to Christianity's distinction between Creator and creation. They insist that God has given "birth to" or has "begotten" nature. Thus, God and the world are one in being.

Professor David Scott of the Virginia Theological Seminary has called this the "Christification" of nature, showing that these theologians (and others) are claiming for nature those attributes that Christians have historically reserved for Jesus Christ.[9] The substantial (or essential) identity of the Father and the Son, which was established at Nicaea and Constantinople, is now being applied to God and nature. If not full-blown pantheism, this monism represents something very close to it. It shares with pantheism its ultimate bad news that robs us of a personal God.[10]

Among the more serious difficulties in the modern reversions to ancient paganism is what happens to a society that believes God and nature are one. McFague and others, while conceding that there is evil in the world, claim that evil is not merely a part of the world but also a part of God. Thus, monism dulls the ethical imperative that makes it possible for a just society to distinguish between good and evil. It leaves the individual, who does so distinguish, in the position of being the judge of God. We must decide what is good in God and what is evil in God. Once more we are well described by Niebuhr's dictum: "In the beginning God created man in his own image and ever since we have sought to return the compliment." The ultimate arrogance of reversing our relationship with God becomes a nurture of self-righteousness without the hope of repentance and change, without the hope of justice that corrects our waywardness, and without even the need for mercy.

This monistic identification of God with everything is not new. Carl Jung's *Answer to Job* insists that since there is both light and darkness, goodness and evil in God, we must distinguish them, accepting light and goodness and rejecting darkness and evil. Thus we are of necessity the judges of God. These views did not originate with Jung; they have represented popular religion since ancient times. Monist teachings have been historically a part of pantheism but they are now presented to us by their adherents as "new" and part of our evolving sophistication. It is valuable to learn from C.S. Lewis how old and primitive they are.

> Pantheism is congenial to our minds not because it is the final stage in a slow process of enlightenment, but because it is almost as old as we are. It may even be the most primitive of all religions. . . . It is immemorial in India. The Greeks rose above it only at their peak, in the thought of Plato and Aristotle; their successors relapsed into the great Pantheistic system of the Stoics. Modern Europe escaped it only while she remained predominantly Christian; with Giordano Bruno and Spinoza it

returned. With Hegel it became almost the agreed philosophy of highly educated people, while the more popular Pantheism of Wordsworth, Carlyle and Emerson conveyed the same doctrine to those on a slightly lower cultural level. So far from being the final religious refinement, Pantheism is in fact the permanent natural bent of the human mind; the permanent ordinary level below which man sometimes sinks, under the influence of priest-craft and superstition, but above which his own unaided efforts can never raise him for very long. Platonism and Judaism, and Christianity (which has incorporated both) have proved the only things capable of resisting it. It is the attitude into which the human mind automatically falls when left to itself. No wonder we find it congenial. If "religion" means simply what man says about God, and not what God does about man, then Pantheism almost *is* religion. And "religion" in that sense has, in the long run, only one really formidable opponent—namely Christianity.[11]

Pantheism, "the permanent natural bent of the human mind," is the corollary to the human factor we have seen in the rise of heresies that appeal to and nurture the worst aspects of our natures. This human factor is even more operative in dealing with these recrudescent pagan religions than with the perennial heresies. The guidelines of Christian orthodoxy are indispensable in recognizing and responding to these ancient religions, which are now reappearing after lying dormant in the West for centuries. Spokespersons for these contemporary revivals see themselves as departing from traditional orthodoxy, but in many cases their reaction is not against orthodoxy but against one of the heresies.

Mary Daly's widely quoted dictum: "Since God is male, the male is God"[12] has been the rallying cry of many feminist theologians who have sought to repudiate traditional orthodox language about God in order to overcome what they see as the patriarchal, tribal, oppressive, authoritarian, and misogynist history of the church. These assumptions have led Mary Daly to renounce Christianity, Carter Heyward to claim about Christianity that only "a spiritually vacuous imagination would have dreamt up such a god," and Daphne Hampton to claim that "feminism represents the death-knell of Christianity as a viable religious option."[13]

As a professional theologian, Daly can not be ignorant of the fact that Christian orthodoxy has never taught that "God is male." In fact, in speaking against the pagan deities who were male, female, and syzygies (hermaphrodite divinities), the Christian church insisted that God as Father does not indicate male sexuality, either in the Bible or in central Christian and Jewish traditions, unlike similar language in ancient pagan and Gnostic religions. To this point Roland Frye quotes Hans Küng that this fatherhood symbol "has no sexual implications and has nothing to do with religious paternalism."[14] What Professor Daly is objecting to is not Christian orthodoxy but a pagan distortion of it.

Colin Gunton insists:

> Insofar as the alleged maleness of Jesus has been used as the basis for arguments excluding women from playing a full part in the ministry of the church, there has been, I believe, a denial of the gospel not of some supposed inherent human or female rights.[15] The fatherhood of God has nothing to do with maleness but with patterns of relationality revealed and realized in Jesus.[16]

We have seen in a previous chapter the poignant example of the person who has trouble with the theology of the crucifixion, which is seen only as an abusive act of a father toward his child. What is objected to is precisely the Arian heresy, not orthodox Christianity of the creeds in which "substantial" or essential identity of Father and Son is established. Victims of abuse can be in double jeopardy as victims of the cruelty of the Arian heresy. This person's cry says something unfortunate about the church's lack of concern for sound teaching and underscores the need in every age to present orthodox teaching afresh to avoid such cruel results of heresy.

Similarly, the attempts by McFague, Jantzen, and others to

deny the distinctions between God and nature is a reaction to a heresy rather than to orthodox Christianity. David Scott wisely perceives their legitimate concern—to correct a heavy, one-sided, transcendent emphasis that seemed to exclude God from the world. They are attempting to establish an immanent sense of God with and in nature. However, these attempts are not a reaction to orthodoxy, which always balances God's transcendence with God's indwelling immanence and sees this divine action and presence in nature. Deism, not Christianity, gives us a picture of an absent, non-immanent watchmaker, aloof from the world and its working.

In his widely popular book *Honest to God,* J.A.T. Robinson attempted to replace the traditional transcendent image of God with one that depicts God as the ground of being rather than some far off and unbelievable deity "up there." His insistence that modern people could no longer believe in a god who dressed up "like Father Christmas" was a reaction not to orthodox Christianity but to the heresy of Sabellianism.

Relinquishing Christianity because one only sees it in the guise of some heresy is a long tradition. The philosopher David Hume wrote a letter in 1739 stating, "Upon the whole, I desire to take my catalogue of Virtues from *Cicero's Offices,* not from *The Whole Duty of Man.*" He had abandoned Christianity altogether by the time he was twenty. James Boswell asked him if he were not religious when he was young. "He said he was, and he used to read *The Whole Duty of Man;* that he made an abstract from the catalogue offices at the end of it, and examined himself by this."[17]

We have noticed in the chapter on Nestorianism how this widely popular devotional work is a stark example of the Adoptionist heresy and something of Hume's reaction to it. We see further what effect this teaching had on one of the seminal minds of the eighteenth century. *The Whole Duty of Man,* published in 1657, was a standard devotional guide and recommended by church leaders over the next two centuries. It clearly reflects the Adoptionist heresy with the characteristics we have seen in Pelagianism and Nestorianism. Any benefits of Christ will flow to us only "on condition we perform our part of the covenant" which is obedience "to all God's commands." This devotional book contains virtually none of the good news of the Gospel. It is presented as though the threat of hell is adequate medicine for sin. The problem is seen to be that people "do not heartily believe that sin will damn them." The solution, to help sinners "to apprehend their damnation and to grasp its nearness," is not the Gospel.[18]

The righteousness necessary for salvation, as seen in Galatians, Romans and Ephesians, is the righteousness of Christ. In *The Whole Duty of Man* the righteousness necessary for forgiveness as well as salvation, the cruel teaching which nurtured Hume's childhood, is one's own charity and devotion. These latter "spiritual graces our souls must be clothed with . . . [are] that Wedding Garment" without which we cannot come to the Lord's feast. (Who would not rather read Cicero?) This seventeenth century reappearance of Adoptionism is an explicit contrast to the orthodox Anglicanism of John Donne and Richard Hooker who saw the "Wedding Garment" as, in Donne's words, the "garments of the Elder Brother" (As Jacob received the blessing of his father Isaac by wearing the garments of his elder brother, Esau, so we now receive the blessing of the Father by wearing the garments of our Elder Brother, Christ.)

It is tempting to speculate what effect the quite different good news in the orthodoxy of Hooker and Donne might have had on David Hume. Both John and Charles Wesley, who had also been nurtured in the Adoptionist teachings of *The Whole Duty of Man* and similar literature, each independently discovered St. Paul's teaching in Galatians (Charles on May 21, 1738) and Romans (John on May 24) that corrected the Adoptionism that had previously characterized their understanding of Christianity. Their life-changing experiences occurred in the very year before Hume wrote the above-mentioned letter justifying his abandonment of Christianity on the grounds that he preferred to take his virtues from Cicero than from *The Whole Duty of Man.*

In perusing Hume's six volume history of England one finds nothing that would lead one to believe he had any grasp of the orthodox Christianity of Thomas Cranmer, Richard Hooker, Lancelot Andrewes, or John Donne, the great Anglicans of the sixteenth and seventeenth centuries, that would have given him something of the gospel that the Wesleys had discovered in Luther's commentaries on Romans and Galatians.

The Adoptionism with which the church struggled in the early centuries is indeed perennial. We have also seen that Adolf von Harnack, the great church historian, was a committed and self-conscious Adoptionist who believed that it was enough for Jesus Christ to be a heroic example for us to follow. It was not important that Christ died to destroy sin and rose again to destroy death; his teaching and the example of his life are enough.

Harnack taught that we are, by nature and creation, children of God. He separated the universal Fatherhood of God and the Brotherhood of Man from the fact that God established this Fatherhood and Brotherhood in the action of Jesus Christ. The teaching of scripture and the church, that God's Fatherhood is a new relationship given to us in the action of Christ, is now, according to Harnack, not a gift but a right and an entitlement of everyone, a claim upon God that eliminates any need for Christian humility in, and gratitude for, our adoption.

This separation of Fatherhood from the Trinity and from the loving and dependent relationship disclosed between Father and Son is the very target that some feminist theologians are actually attacking when they abhor the masculine language for God in scripture. Patriarchal misogynist inferences can be drawn from the masculine language for God only if one separates them from the Passion and crucifixion of Christ. The humble, pouring out, self-sacrificing action of God in his only begotten Son, his life of servanthood and freely chosen death brings to naught all masculine arrogance and pretension. The unique Fatherhood, given us in the costly life, death, and resurrection of Jesus, judges, informs, and transforms all fatherhoods (not the other way around).

Janice Martin Soskice shows how the trinitarian context for "Fatherhood" (which Harnack excluded) is the result of the graceful repudiation of authoritarian and patriarchal oppression in society and church by the male, Jesus, laying down those distortions in his crucifixion. Authoritarian and patriarchal oppression is part of that sin Jesus bore on the cross and buried in his death. Soskice uses a theme from Paul Ricoeur that in the crucifixion the only-begotten Son of the Father is found the "death of separated transcendence."[19] One is left, not without God, but without the separated God. We are now "bold" to call him "Father," not because of some innate right based on creation, but because of the costly gift of God in Christ whereby we are adopted as sons and daughters. The outpouring of Christ empties Fatherhood of all against which feminists are justly reacting.

We should be objecting not to orthodox Christian faith but to the renaming and de-trinitizing of Fatherhood by the Harnacks of the nineteenth century. Christians must make sure that the orthodoxy they proclaim is truly the "right opinion" and not another heresy lurking under the garments of "conservatism" or some other term that the unwary will assume to be orthodox. One can but open that most prestigious of scholarly aids, *The Oxford Dictionary of the Christian Church,* to discover a pernicious example of lingering Adoptionism in the article on "Moral Theology" that claims moral theology to be the "science of Christian conduct treating of God as man's last end, and of *the means by which He may be attained"*[1958 edition, italics mine]. Moral theology of Christian orthodoxy tells us not how to follow moral rules in order to attain God, but how we respond by ethical behavior in gratitude to our having been recipients of Christ's sacrifice for our sin and the victory over death.

The guidelines and boundaries set by the great councils and creeds are among the most urgently needed bases of the Christian faith today. In an age that often seems to value skepticism and criticism over faithfulness and gratitude, it is refreshing indeed to encounter Professor Roland Frye's appreciation of what has been given us.

> The formulation of the Christian doctrine of the Trinity is one of the most impressive intellectual achievements in human history, whatever else it may be. It involved analyses of at least equal sophistication of those of present-day astrophysics and physical theory, and it achieved coherence of theological meaning while preserving the divine mystery. Five or six centuries were required for the full development of this careful, nuanced, and balanced formulation to preserve and present theologically the three persons whom Christians encounter as divine, without falling into polytheism, but maintaining a single and undivided godhead: Father, Son, and Holy Spirit.[20]

We must, however, recall that orthodoxy has earned for itself much opprobrium and disapproval. The incomparable formularies so indispensable to the church's integrity in both past and present must never again be tolerated as vestments under which to hide authoritarianism, coercion, misogyny, or uncritical adulation of the past.

Recalling the root stem of the word dogma, which comes from the word *dokein,* meaning "to seem," it would behoove us to have a humble tone in our witness no matter how justified our convictions. This duty of orthodox persons is not merely a matter of etiquette but of dogma, the dogma of the incarnate God whose self-revelation was made to those who did not believe in order that they might believe, who went to Golgotha rather than coerce, who accepted betrayal and apparently final defeat in order that the Easter victory be God's and God's

alone. This dogma means that those who are genuinely orthodox must likewise be willing "not to win" while they are being
faithful.

Next to sin itself, the chief reason for orthodoxy's bad name
was the use, after the Constantinian victory, of the state's power
to enforce orthodoxy (which must be seen to be a contradiction
in terms). Thus, the dream of any return to Christendom, whereby society and culture embody the very structures and authority of orthodoxy, should not obscure the present providential
opportunity to allow God to wring out any lingering poisonous
arrogance in the fabric of what seems to be orthodoxy.

The fact that orthodoxy has been at times badly represented
ought not to obscure the larger fact that the essence of Christianity is resisted by a human desire for a religious justification
of our self-centeredness, on the one hand, and for a religious
encouragement of escape from life, on the other. The good news
of Christ frees us from the prison of self-centeredness with the
gift of an eternal Center and from an escape into death by the
promise of an abundant life.

While heresies nurture these illnesses that scripture calls sin
and death, many would have us believe that they are daring
new advances in truth. Heresies are not "errors of understanding but errors of the will." Sound doctrine is indispensable to
Christian faith, "a rectitude of the heart," and the saving knowledge of God, Father, Son and Holy Spirit. The consequent fruit is
love, joy, peace, patience, kindness, goodness, faithfulness, gentleness, self-control; against such there is no law (Gal. 5:22-23).

Notes

Introduction

1. Honor Matthews, *The Primal Curse: The Myth of Cain and Abel in the Theatre* (London: Chatto and Winders, 1967), 14.

2. W. B. Yeats, "The Second Coming."

3. Lesslie Newbigin, *The Gospel in a Pluralist Society* (Grand Rapids, MI: Eerdmans, 1989), 22.

4. Jeremy Taylor, *The Liberty of Prophesying*, 461.

5. *The Complete Works of Samuel Taylor Coleridge,* ed. Professor Shedd, (New York: Harper and Brothers, 1876). Vol. V, 172 .

Chapter One: Short Beds and Narrow Blankets

1. Kenneth Clark, *Civilisation* (London: B.B.C., 1961), 29.

2. *Book of Common Prayer* (New York: Church Hymnal Corp., 1979), l68.

3. Robert Frost, "Kitty Hawk," *In the Clearing,* (New York: Holt Rinehart, 1962), 49.

4. Dorothee Sölle, *Suffering* (London: DLT, 1976), 131. It is perhaps Professor Sölle's profound grasp of this truth, and her abhorrence of its denial in *conventional* Christianity, that has driven her to such extremes as to deny any transcendence in Christianity.

5. St. Augustine, *City of God*, XIV, 13.

6. William Porcher DuBose, *The Ecumenical Councils*, 4th ed. (Edinburgh: T. and T. Clark, Ltd, 1911), 57.

7. Ronald Grant, quoted in program for "Mama, I Want to Sing" production, Gaillard Municipal Auditorium, Charleston, SC, March, 1992.

8. R. A. Norris, Jr. ed. *The Christological Controversy* (Philadelphia: Fortress Press, 1980), 33-47.

Chapter Two: Attacks on Christian Faith

1. *De Bello Gallico* III, 18.

2. Irenaeus, *Against Heresies* III xvii. 1.

3. Ibid., V. vii. 1.

4. Ibid., I,11.

5. C. S. Lewis, *The Allegory of Love* (New York: Oxford University Press, 1958)

Chapter Three: The Trinity

1. Collect for Trinity Sunday, *Canadian Book of Common Prayer*, 1928.

2. A modern example of this monistic resolution is "process theology," which attempts to overcome the charge of being a new version of impersonal pantheism by claiming the word "panentheism" instead. It is a theology derived from the thought of the philosopher Alfred North Whitehead (1861-1947). A pert-

inent comment on this endeavor is found in the title of a book by Stephen Lee Ely, *The Religious Availability of Whitehead's God* (Madison: University of Wisconsin Press). The answer is: his god is not available.

3. *Sewanee Theological Review,* Pentecost, 1992, Vol. 35:3, 231.

Chapter Four: Arianism: The Three Deities

1. William Porcher DuBose, *The Ecumenical Councils,* 4th ed. (Edinburgh: T. and T. Clark, Ltd, 1911), 77.

2. *Book of Common Prayer* (1928), 577.

3. C. S. Lewis, "Introduction," in *The Incarnation of the Word of God,* transl. A Religious of C.S.M.V., S.Th. (New York: The Macmillan Company, 1947), 11.

4. *The Incarnation of the Word of God,* xx. 1.

5. Ibid. liv. 3.

6. Philip Turner, *Sex, Money and Power: An Essay in Christian Social Ethics* (Cambridge, MA: Cowley Press, 1985), 18-19.

Chapter Five: The Cappadocians

1. J.W.C. Wand, *A History of the Early Church to A.D. 500* (London: Methuen and Co. Ltd., 1937), 174.

2. G.L. Prestige, *God in Patristic Thought,* 113. Prestige claims that there is no evidence of such use of the term *prosopon* by the Sabellians. However it was the secular term for "mask" or "role" and, therefore, cause for the Eastern theologians to prefer *hypostasis.*

3. Gerald Bray, *Creeds, Councils and Christ* (Downers Grove, IL: Inter-Varsity Press, 1984), 202.

4. For an important contribution to this whole subject of "person" see E.L. Mascall, *Theology and the Gospel of Christ* (London: S.P.C.K., 1977) and his *Whatever Happened to the Human Mind?* (London: S.P.C.K., 1980). Also see Jean Galot, *Who is Christ?* (Gregorian University Press, 1981) and *Persons, Divine and Human,* ed. Christoph Schwöbel and Colin Gunton, (Edinburgh: T. and T. Clark, 1991).

Chapter Six: Apollinarianism

1. *For the Time Being* (New York: Random House, 1944), 77-78.

2. Gregory of Nyssa, *Against the Eunomians,* 2.10.

3. There is some uncertainty whether Apollinarius himself believed that human nature was comprised of two or three components, but what is agreed upon is that one of them, the human mind or spirit or soul, was replaced by the divinity of Christ. By extension, Apollinarianism has been seen to be any heresy that sees redemption as replacing or destroying anything essentially human.

4. Paul Tillich, *Systematic Theology,* vol. III, 122.

5. Apollinarius, *On the Faith of the Incarnation.*

6. Theodore of Mopsuestia, *On the Incarnation,* 15.3.

7. The phrase "and the son" (filioque) was not a part of the original creed but added in later centuries in the Western church. It is a source of disagreement today between Eastern Orthodox and Western churches.

8. Quoted by William Porcher DuBose, *The Ecumenical Councils,* 174.

9. Ibid., 173-74

Chapter Seven: Nestorianism: The Train of Salvation Does Not Stop for Sinners

1. Jeremy Taylor, *Works,* ed. Heber, V. 64.

2. Ibid., 87.

3. C. F. Allison, *The Rise of Moralism* (Harrisburg, PA: Morehouse, 1984), 151.

4. Ibid., 152.

5. Ibid., 151.

6. Alasdair MacIntyre, *Whose Justice? Which Rationality?* (South Bend, IN: University of Notre Dame Press, 1988), 282.

7. Richard Hooker, *Of the Laws of Ecclesiastical Polity,* Bk VI, iii, 3.

8. *Coleridge on the Seventeenth Century,* ed. R. F. Brinkley, (Durham, NC: Duke University Press, 1955), 328-29.

9. Two apparent exceptions are: "you were free in regard to righteousness . . ." (Rom. 6:20) which is obviously ironic, and (1 Pet. 2:16) "Live as free men, yet without using your freedom as a pretext for evil" which is addressed to those in Christ that they not use their claim to true liberty to fall back into sin, which would be bondage.

Chapter Eight: Eutychianism: The Religious Withering of Humanity

1. Hooker, *Ecclesiastical Polity,* Bk V, 54,10.

2. *Book of Common Prayer,* 864.

3. Quoted in Wand, *The History of the Early Church to AD 500,* 242.

4. It is significant that these two critics of Chalcedon, Anthony T. Hanson and Norman Pittenger, in calling it Monophysite have themselves admitted that their perspective is that of

Nestorianism. Anthony T. Hanson, *Grace and Truth* (London: S.P.C.K., 1975), 106.
On the other hand, Hanson's criticism of Pannenberg's narrow historical base (p. 109-11) is exceptionally well taken and would seem to continue that contribution of Antiochene emphasis which although inadequate itself, nevertheless corrects the unhistorical tendency of Alexandrians.

5. Bray, *Creeds, Councils and Christ*. "Detractors of Chalcedon, who claim that the council never got to grips with the true manhood of Jesus, are apt to overlook this later development, and as a result their perspective is distorted. We cannot understand Chalcedon unless we are prepared to get to grips with the way it was explained and defended in the East after 451." 168.

6. *Meister Eckhardt,* compiled by Franz Pfeiffer, transl. by C. deB. Evans, (Snowmass Village, CO: Gordon Press, 1977), Vol. 1, 48.

7. Evelyn Underhill, *Worship* (New York: Harper, 1936) 3,6.

8. Douglas John Hall, *Imaging God* (Grand Rapids, MI: Eerdmans, 1986), 228.

Chapter Nine: A Rectitude of the Heart

1. Colin E. Gunton, *Enlightenment and Alienation: An Essay Towards a Trinitarian Theology* (Grand Rapids, MI: Eerdmans, 1985), 154.

2. G. K. Chesterton, *St. Francis of Assisi* (New York: Doubleday), 154.

3. H.O.J. Brown, *Heresies* (Garden City, New York: Doubleday, 1984), 170.

4. *The Complete Works of Samuel Taylor Coleridge* (New York: Harper, 1876), Vol.V, 172.

5. Adolf von Harnack, *History of Dogma,* Vol. 1, 711 ff. A convenient summary of Harnack's views can be found in Brown's *Heresies,* 97.

6. Janice Martin Soskice, "Can a Feminist Call God 'Father'?" in *Speaking the Christian God: The Holy Trinity and the Challenge of Feminism,* ed. Alvin Kimel (Grand Rapids, MI: Eerdmans, 1992) 88.

7. *Time* magazine, November 12, 1979.

8. *Theological Freedom and Social Responsibility,* ed. Stephen Bayne (New York: Seabury Press, 1967), 22.

9. "I am appalled at . . . Dr. George Carey's . . . use of the ugly word 'heresy.' I thought this word had now been dropped from theological discourse." *The Daily Telegraph,* Friday, March 1, 1991.

Chapter Ten: Orthodoxy and Pagan Religions Revived

1. James W. Sire, *The Universe Next Door,* 2nd ed. (Downers Grove, IL: Inter-Varsity Press, 1988), 204.

2. Shirley MacLaine's books include: *Don't Fall Off the Mountain, Dancing in the Light, It's All in the Playing,* and *Going Within.* For a critique see *The Universe Next Door* by James W. Sire or *Unmasking the New Age* by Douglas R. Groothius (Downers Grove, IL: Inter-Varsity Press, 1986), 15.

3. A valuable critique of this widely influential movement may be found in Paul Vitz's *Psychology as Religion: The Cult of Self Worship* (Grand Rapids, MI: Eerdmans, 1977).

4. Lesslie Newbigin, *Truth to Tell: The Gospel as Public Trust* (Grand Rapids, MI: Eerdmans, 1991), 62.

5. G.K. Chesterton, *Orthodoxy* (New York: John Lane and Co., 1919), 136.

6. Carl Gustof Jung, *Psychology of the Unconscious,* 52.

7. M. Scott Peck, *The Road Less Traveled* (New York: Simon and Schuster, 1978), 282-83.

8. Groothius, *Unmasking the New Age*, 153.

9. David Scott, "Creation as Christ," in *Speaking the Christian God*, 237ff.

10. For an excellent critique of the monist beliefs in J. A. T. Robinson, John Spong and Sallie McFague see Stephen Smith's essay "Worldview, Language and Radical Feminism" in *Speaking the Christian God*.

11. C. S. Lewis, *Miracles* (New York: Macmillan, 1947), 84-85.

12. Mary Daly, "The Qualitative Leap Beyond Patriarchal Religion," *Quest* 1, 1974, 21.

13. Carter Heyward, *Touching Our Strength* (San Francisco: Harper, 1989), 81. Daphne Hampson, *Theology and Feminism* (Oxford: Basil Blackwell, 1990), 1.

14. Roland Frye, "Language for God and Feminist Language," in *Speaking the Christian God*, 20.

15. Colin Gunton, "Proteus and Procustes," in *Speaking the Christian God*, 77.

16. Ibid., 78.

17. Quoted in A. MacIntyre, *Whose Justice? Which Rationality?* (Notre Dame, IN: Notre Dame Press, 1988), 282-83.

18. Allison, *The Rise of Moralism*, 152.

19. Soskice, "Can a Feminist Call God 'Father'?," in *Speaking the Christian God*, 91.

20. Frye, 22.

Bibliography

The most easily available series of original sources in English are *The Ante-Nicene Fathers* and *The Nicene and Post-Nicene Fathers* published by Eerdmans.

For specialized items on the classical writers:
Quasten, J. *Patrology.* 3 vols. Utrecht: Spectrum, 1950-60.

Among the best one-volume comprehensive surveys is:
Bray, Gerald. *Creeds, Councils and Christ.* Leicester, England, and Downers Grove, IL: Inter-Varsity Press, 1984.

One of the clearest and simplest accounts of the classical heresies is:
Wand, J.W.C., *The Four Great Heresies.* London: Mowbray, 1957.

An old but unsurpassed classic is:
DuBose, William Porcher. *The Ecumenical Councils.* 4th ed. Edinburgh: T. and T. Clark Ltd., 1911.

Other recommended works:
Brown, Harold O. J. *Heresies.* Garden City, New York: Doubleday, 1984.
Galot, J. *Who Is Christ?* Gregorian University Press, 1981.

Gunton, Colin E. *Enlightenment and Alienation: An Essay Toward a Trinitarian Theology.* Grand Rapids, MI: Eerdmans, 1985.

Hanson, R. P. C. *The Search for the Christian Doctrine of God: The Arian Controversy 318-381.* Edinburgh: T. and T. Clark, 1988.

Hill, W. J. *The Three-Personed God: The Trinity as a Mystery of Salvation.* Washington: Catholic University of America Press, 1982.

Jenson, Robert. *The Triune Identity.* Philadelphia: Fortress, 1982.

Kelly, J. N. D. *Early Christian Creeds.* A. and C. Black, 1977.

———*Early Christian Doctrines.* 5th ed. A. and C. Black, 1977.

Lee, Philip J. *Against the Protestant Gnostics.* New York: Oxford University Press, 1987.

Lonergan, B. *The Way to Nicea.* London: Darton, Longman and Todd, 1976.

Mascall, E. L. *Theology and the Gospel of Christ.* London: S.P.C.K., 1977.

Schwöbel, Christoph and Colin Gunton, ed. *Persons Divine and Human,* Edinburgh: T. and T. Clark, 1991.

Sturch, Richard. *The Word and the Christ: An Essay in Analytic Christology.* New York: Oxford University Press, 1991.

Torrance, T. F. *The Trinitarian Faith: The Evangelical Theology of the Ancient Catholic Church.* Edinburgh: T. and T. Clark, Ltd., 1988.

Two helpful books on Christianity and alternative world views in contemporary religions and cults are:

Geisler, Norman and William Watkins. *Worlds Apart, A Handbook on World Views.* 2nd ed. Grand Rapids, MI: Baker Book House, 1989.

Sire, J. W. *The Universe Next Door.* Downers Grove, IL: Inter-Varsity Press, 1988.

Two important critiques of contemporary assaults on the doctrine of the Trinity are:

Bloesch, Donald G. *The Battle for the Trinity.* Ann Arbor, MI: Vine Books, 1985.

Kimel, Alvin, ed. *Speaking the Christian God: The Holy Trinity and the Challenge of Feminism.* Grand Rapids, MI: Eerdmans, 1992.

Index

Abel, 46
Abraham, 72, 114, 130-31, 161
Adam, 39, 53
Adoptionism, 32-34, 35, 39-47, 74, 103, 120, 125, 159, 174-75
Against Heresies (Irenaeus), 51-52
Albigensians, 62-63, 65
Alexander, Bishop, 85, 88
Ambrose, St., 133
American Piety (Glock and Stark), 156
Andrewes, Lancelot, 175
Anglican Church, 16, 93, 140
Answer to Job (Jung), 170
Antioch, Synod, 119
Anti-Semitism, 51
Apollinarianism, 105-17, 121, 133
Apollinarius, 105-7, 109, 119

Aquinas, Thomas, 136
Arianism, 81-94, 95, 96, 99
Aristotle, 170
Arius, 18, 19, 83-88, 107, 120
Arnold, Matthew, 157
Athanasius, 18, 19, 88-94, 96, 99, 102, 107, 116, 142, 151, 154
Atonement, 87, 122
Auden, W. H., 105
Augustine, St., 39, 62, 114, 130, 132-37
Aurelius, Marcus, Emperor, 70

Bannister, Roger, 31
Baptism, 40, 41, 112
Barabbas, 112
Barth, Karl, 19
Basil of Caesarea, 95
Basilides of Egypt, 55
Bayne, Stephen, Bishop, 69

Berger, Peter, 19
Bergler, Edmund, 59
Bernard of Clairvaux, 63, 65, 136, 148
Beyond Freedom and Dignity (Skinner), 108
Bismarck, O. E. L., von, 21
Bogomiles, 62
Book of Common Prayer, 60, 127, 132
Boswell, James, 173
Bray, Gerald, 100, 146
Brown, Harold O. J., 156
Browning, Robert, 59, 60
Bruno, Giordano, 170
Buddha, 62
Bultmann, Rudolf, 19
Burgess, Anthony, 108
Burkitt, F. C., 62

Caesar, Julius, 49
Call to Heresy (Can de Weyer), 18
Calvin, John, 136
Canon of scripture, 26, 51, 65
Cappodocians, 95-104, 154
Carlyle, 171
Chalcedon, Council, 54, 140, 142, 146
Chesterton, G. K., 155, 167, 169
Christianity reduced to religion of law, 34
Christology, 54, 136, 149
Christian Science, 30

Cicero, 175
Cicero's Offices, 173
Clockwork Orange (Burgess), 108
Coleridge, Samuel Taylor, 23, 34, 131, 148, 158-59
Constantine, 27
Constantinople, Council, 86, 93, 98, 105
Councils, ecumenical, 20, 73, 93
Cranmer, Thomas, Archbishop, 127, 136, 160, 175
Creed of Nicaea and Constantinople, 115
Creeds, 49
Crucifix, 29
Cyril of Alexandria, 121, 140, 142

Daly, Mary, 171-72
Dante Alighieri, 109. 130
David, 46
De Incarnatione (Athanasius), 8
Dioscorus of Alexandria, 141, 144
Divine Comedy (Dante), 130
Docetism, 27-31, 34, 35-39, 56, 109, 111-12, 136, 157
Donatism, 115
Donne, John, 174, 175
DuBose, William Porcher, 35, 44, 81, 116, 143

Eastern Orthodox churches, 16, 93, 140
Ebionism, 31-34
Eckhardt, Meister, 147
Eddy, Mary Baker, 30
Elijah, 159
Eliot, T. S., 157
Emerson, R. W., 171
Entropy, 22
Ephesus, Council, 129, 137, 161
Epiphanius, 51
Erasmus, 130
Esau, 174
Escape From Freedom (Fromm), 108
Eutyches, 140-41, 144
Eutychianism, 139-51
Eve, 39, 105
Exemplarism, 40

Faith of a Heretic (Kaufmann), 18
Fear No Evil (Watson), 150
Flavian of Constantinople, 141-42
Flesh, 110
Flight, 35
Fox, Matthew, 169
Fromm, Erich, 108
Frost, Robert, 36-37
Frye, Roland, 172, 177

Glock, Charles, 156-57
Gnosticism, 53, 55-61, 166

Goodspeed, E. J., 61
Gregory of Nazianzus, 95
Gregory of Nyssa, 95-96
Green, Bryan, Canon, 44-45
Groothius, Douglas, 168
Gunton, Colin, 153, 172

Hadrian, Emperor, 70
Hall, Douglas John, 151
Hammond, Henry, 43
Hampton, Daphne, 172
Hanson, Anthony, 146
Harnack, Adolf, von, 35, 44, 159-60, 175-76
Hegel, G. W. F., 171
Heresy, 17-18, 27, 46; and human will, 34
Heretical Imperative (Berger), 19
Heyward, Carter, 171
Hilary of Poitiers, 116
Homoiousios, 86, 122
Homoousios, 86-88, 91, 93, 96, 106, 122
Honest to God (Robinson), 173
Hooker, Richard, 126, 139, 174, 175
Hume, David, 126, 173-74
Huntington, William Reed, 30
Hypostasis, 97, 145

Ibsen, Heinrich, 158
Idealism, 37

Idolatry, 103-4
If This Be Heresy (Pike), 18
Incarnation, 144
Independence, 91-92
Inge, Dean, 148
Irenaeus, 51-55, 73, 102, 104, 116, 154
Isaac, 72, 114, 174
Islam, 29

Jackson, Andrew, 32
Jacob, 72, 98, 174
James, St., 57
Jantzen, Grace, 169, 172
Jenkins, David, Bishop, 78
Jesus Christ: divine, not human, 27-29; human, not divine, 25, 31; human and divine, 53-54; moral union of divinity and humanity, 121; no human mind, 107; two persons, 123
John, St., 57, 60
Joseph (New Testament), 31
Joseph (Old Testament), 46, 98, 161
Judaizers, 39-40
Julian, Emperor, 105-6
Jung, Carl Gustaf, 167-68, 170
Justin, St., 51

Kairology, 127
Kaufmann, Walter, 18, 19
Kazantzakis, Nikos, 135-36

Keller, Helen, 112
Kübler-Ross, Elisabeth, 162
Küng, Hans, 172

Last Temptation of Christ (Kazantzakis), 135
Lehmann, Paul, 86
Leo I, Pope, 142, 147
Leonides, 83
Leontius, 147
Lewis, C. S., 63, 88, 170
Logos, 74, 85, 107, 109
Love, 37, 45, 63, 77, 91-92
Love in the Western World (de Rougemont), 63
Luke, St., 50, 161
Luther, Katie, 114
Luther, Martin, 114, 130, 136, 175
Lutheran Church, 16, 140

Macedonianism, 115
MacLaine, Shirley, 166
Macquarrie, John, 163
Macrina, 96
Magus, Simon, 55
Mani, 62
Manichaeism, 61-66, 132
Manson, Charles, 168-69
Marcion, 19, 50-51, 53, 55, 65, 103
Marcionism, 55
Marriage, 64
Marx, Karl, 112
Mary, 31, 121, 143, 161

Mary Magdalene, 135
Maslow, Abraham, 166
Matthew, St., 161
Matthews, Honor, 15
McFague, Sallie, 169-70, 172
Melito of Sardis, 46
Messiah, 98
Methodist Church, 16, 93, 140
Monarchianism, 73-79; Modalistic and Dynamic, 74
Monasticism, 38
Monica, 133
Monism, 76, 166, 168-70
Monophysitism, 107, 140, 144
Monroe, Marilyn, 71
Montanism, 52, 55
Montanus, 51-52, 53
Montfort, Simon de, 63
Moses, 41, 46, 84, 131, 159
Mysticism, 147-48

Neoplatonism, 51, 145, 163
Nestorianism, 119-37, 173
Nestorius, 120, 122, 132
New Age, 30, 165, 166
Newbigin, Lesslie, 20, 167
Nicaea, Council, 73, 85, 93, 96
Nicodemus, 129
Niebuhr, Reinhold, 101, 148, 170

O'Neill, Eugene, 36, 158
Ontology, 129
Origen, 83-84, 103
Orthodoxy, 18-23, 27, 34, 45, 70, 102-3, 155, 157, 164, 178
Ousia, 97-98

Pantheism, 76, 170-71
Paracelsus, 59
Patripassianism, 74
Paul, St., 33, 42, 50, 60, 61, 108, 137, 146, 155, 174
Paul of Samosata, 44, 120, 136
Paulicians, 62
Peck, Scott, 168
Pelagianism, 111, 130, 158
Pelagius, 130, 132
Perfection, 43
Persona, 99-100
Peter, Bishop, 96
Peter, St., 26, 57, 108
Physis, 123, 140-41
Pike, James, Bishop, 18, 19, 49
Pittenger, Norman, 146
Pius, Antonius, Emperor, 70
Plato, 163, 170
Pneumaticism, 35, 57
Presley, Elvis, 71
Principles of Self-Damage (Bergler), 59
Process theology, 180 (ch. 3, n. 2)

Prosopon, 99, 101, 121, 124,
181 (ch. 5, n. 2)
Psilanthropism, 120
Pulcheria, 142

Recapitulation, 52-53
Redemption, 42
Reformed Church, 16, 33,
93, 140
Ricoeur, Paul, 176
Righteousness, 33-34, 42
Risk, 38
Road Less Traveled (Peck),
168
Robinson, J. A. T., 173
Rogers, Carl, 166
Roman Catholic Church, 16,
33, 93, 140
Rougemont, Denis de, 63

Sabellianism, 96-97, 99, 173
Sabellius, 74-75, 83
Sarx, 60-61, 63
Schleiermacher, Friedrich,
19
Schweitzer, Albert, 37
Scott, David, 169, 173
Second Coming, 51, 52
Self-centeredness, 40
Self-sacrifice, 100
Sermon on the Mount, 42-43
Shakespeare, William, 132
Simon of Cyrene, 29, 55
Sire, James W., 165
Skinner, B. F., 108

Socianism, 33, 136, 147, 158
Socinus, Fausto and Lelio, 33
Socrates, 163
Sölle, Dorothee, 38, 180 (ch.
3, n. 4)
Soskice, Janice Martin, 176
Soteriology, 54, 89
Spinoza, Baruch, 170
Stark, Rodney, 156-57
Subordinationism, 87
Substantia, 99, 101
Substantiation, 36-37
Suicide, 63

Tate, Sharon, 168
Taylor, Jeremy, Bishop, 23,
34, 125, 148, 159
Tertullian, 51, 103
Theodore of Mopsuestia,
113, 119-21, 132, 136
Theodosius II, Emperor, 142
Theodotus the Tanner, 44
*Theological Freedom and
Social Responsibilities*
(Bayne), 163
Theotokos, 121, 123
Tillich, Paul, 111
Tome (Pope Leo I), 142, 147
Torrance, James, 139
Trajan, Emperor, 70
Trinity, 54, 67-79, 149
Turner, Philip, 90

Underhill, Evelyn, 147-48
Unitarianism, 136, 147, 158

Valens, Emperor, 96
Valentinus, 56
Van de Weyer, Robert, 18, 19

Washington, George, 160
Watson, David, 150
Wesley, John and Charles,
    174, 175
Whole Duty of Man, 125-27,
    173-75
Williams, Tennessee, 158
Wordsworth, William, 171
Worship, 69, 71, 148
Wrenn, Brian, 153

Yeats, W. B., 15, 157

Zaehner, R. C., 168
Zoroaster, 62